D1180722

BUSES
YEARBOOK 1996

Edited by
STEWART J. BROWN

IAN ALLAN Publishing

Contents

First published 1995

ISBN 0 7110 2351 4

Published by Ian Allan Publishing

an imprint of Ian Allan Ltd, Terminal House, Station Approach, Shepperton, Surrey TW17 8AS. Printed by Ian Allan Printing Ltd, Coombelands House, Coombelands Lane, Addlestone, Weybridge, Surrey KT15 1HY.

Front cover: A Leyland Titan of the Oxford Bus Company seen in Central Oxford in June 1994. *Chris Morrison*

Back cover, top: A Bristol RE in Pennine Blue colours.

Back cover, bottom: Eastern Scottish Leyland Tiger. *Stewart J. Brown*

Ten years of style

Optare was formed in 1985 and in just 10 years has produced a succession of trendsetting body styles. **Stuart Jones** looks at the development of the Leeds-based bus builder.

No body manufacturer has had a greater influence on the appearance of the post-deregulation British bus than Optare. The attractive styling of the City Pacer, Delta and Spectra, in particular, have caught the imagination of bus operators and helped prompt other manufacturers to look again at vehicle styling. Not an insignificant achievement for a company that was born only 10 years ago and began by producing rather unspectacular boxy bodies on Dennis Dominos and Leyland Cubs.

Though the company only came into being in February 1985, its pedigree and that of its workforce stretches back much further. The Crossgates plant in Leeds where Optare is based was previously home to Charles H. Roe Ltd, latterly part of Leyland and from 1949 to 1962 part of the ACV group which included AEC, Crossley, Maudslay and Park Royal. Faced with what it perceived as too much bodybuilding capacity, Leyland Bus had shut the factory in September 1984 and transferred much of the plant and equipment to ECW at Lowestoft. Production of the Leyland Royal Tiger Doyen coach was transferred to Workington.

Russell Richardson had been plant director at Roe but had moved to be production director at Duple prior to the Crossgates closure. With support from the West Yorkshire Enterprise Board and from former Roe employees, many of whom invested their Leyland redundancy money, he led the buyout of the factory from Leyland Bus and Optare was formed. The title Optare was derived from the Greek word for 'to choose' and the company soon set about producing a range of vehicles which offered operators new levels of customer appeal.

By June 1985 the first bus had been completed, one of 14 Dennis Dominos with 33-seat midibus bodies for South Yorkshire Transport. A similar body style was supplied on 15 Leyland Cubs for West Yorkshire PTE in 1986. These were to have very short lives with their original operator, being sold on to a variety of independents during 1987. These first products did not exhibit the stylishness for which Optare was to become known but did provide work while the new products were developed.

Below:
Early Optare products gave no clue to the style revolution which was coming. The bodies built on Leyland Cubs for the West Yorkshire PTE were neat, but plain. Generally similar bodies were built on Dennis Dominos for South Yorkshire Transport.
Stewart J. Brown

Another source of work was surprising given Leyland's reason for closing the plant. West Yorkshire PTE took 15 Olympians with the old Roe style of body, two of which were convertible to open top. A further 27 Olympians were built during 1988 for which the customers included Reading Transport, Cambus and Maidstone Boro' line.

West Yorkshire PTE also took the first minibuses to be built at Crossgates, 15 Freight Rover Sherpa high roof van conversions. Sherpa minicoaches were converted too; the initial demonstration vehicle being supplied to Emblings of Guyhirn. Leeds City Council purchased the first of a considerable number of Optare products in the shape of 12 Dodge S56 series; two Ford R1115s were converted to libraries for Leeds and about 40 ambulances were converted from Renault Master vans for a variety of Health Authorities.

City Pacer

When it came, the first model to employ Optare's philosophy of providing the operator with a stylish total package was something of a sensation. Arguably, no British bus had ever looked as good as the City Pacer and certainly few had as closely resembled the artist's impressions before. The deregulated market which came into operation on 26 October 1986 was a new world in which the minibus was to play a major role and Optare was ready

for it. While most manufacturers were offering van conversions which looked exactly what they were, the City Pacer's rounded contours grabbed the eye and said 'get on board'.

Promoted as 'A jewel in the town... that sparkles in the country', the 6.83m-long City Pacer was mounted on the Volkswagen LT55. It seated 25, had a steel-framed structure and featured easily detachable moulded front and lower side panels. The three-piece screen with the deep, double-curvature centre section gave the driver an excellent view of the road. Optare repositioned the driver's seat, mounting it higher than was standard on the LT55 in order to make ticketing easier, although lady drivers were advised not to wear short skirts. A drawback was the need for mechanics to board the vehicle to carry out routine servicing tasks, but compared with the shortcomings of Transits and Sherpas this was acceptable to a good many operators.

A very early customer was London Buses which went on to take 52 of the type; the start of a relationship which was to see large numbers of Optare products delivered to the capital. Blackpool Transport began its association with Optare by purchasing 35 City Pacers, Leicester stocked its Loughborough-based Trippit fleet with them, Yorkshire Rider had a batch including its 'Magic Rider' coach, Silverline of Merthyr Tydfil had four — at least some of which had tail lifts — South Midlands bought some, and Welwyn Hatfield Line began its operations with a batch of 11

and later bought four more. Cambus and Bebb both bought batches; Cambus subsequently acquiring some ex-Taff Ely examples and KMP Llanberis bought five with catalytic convertors for use on a contract which involved running inside a Welsh mountain! Many smaller operators also bought ones and twos, among them Maun International and Boultons of Cardington, while WDM of Bristol took a non-PSV equipped with sophisticated laser sensors for use on checking the condition of highway surfaces.

In total around 300 City Pacer buses, Inter City Pacer 21-seat coaches and City Pacer IIs were built. The City Pacer II was a later development which offered a Telma Ce30 electric retarder as standard in order to improve brake life. The last were delivered with L registration plates.

StarRider

As the minibus market matured, demand for higher capacity minibuses grew and in July 1987 the StarRider was unveiled. The City Pacer had been exclusively available on the LT55 chassis and the StarRider was offered only on the Mercedes 811D and later the more powerful 814D chassis cowl. Early vehicles had chassis which were specially lengthened by Derwent Vehicles to give a 4.8m wheelbase. Later versions were supplied by Mercedes to these dimensions. The overall length of the vehicle was 8.4m which enabled 33 bus or 29 coach seats to be

fitted. Like the City Pacer the structure was of welded steel tube; unlike it, a hinged bonnet-flap provided access for daily checks.

At the launch, examples were shown in the colours of Boultons of Cardington and Yorkshire Rider. London Buses again liked the design and bought a total of 123 as its SR class. Badgerline bought 24 to replace Bristol RE and LH types, the Berks Bucks Beeline fleet bought 10 and Viscount Travel's first new buses were a quartet of StarRiders with tactile plates next to the doors to identify the vehicles to blind passengers. Yorkshire Traction took some for its own fleet and daughter company Lincolnshire Road Car took one ex-demonstrator and three of the rare StarRider E model which had the standard Mercedes front bonnet arrangement rather than Optare's more streamlined design. Most recent customers have opted for the 814D model for coach use, among them Ralphs, Scan Coaches and Brents. By the end of 1994 around 320 had been supplied, perhaps the oddest being an emergency response unit for Gwent Fire Brigade.

Delta

From the start, Russell Richardson's plan had been for Optare to offer a full range of vehicles to meet the needs of bus operators. Having successfully entered the market with its distinctive minibuses, Optare unveiled its plans for the 11.8m

Top:
The StarRider was based on a Mercedes-Benz chassis and offered greater carrying capacity than the CityPacer. A Badgerline StarRider is seen in central Bristol.
Stewart J. Brown

Middle:
MetroRiders for Wear Buses, part of the Go-Ahead group, under construction at Crossgate works.
Stuart Jones

Bottom:
MetroRider development. In the foreground an Optare-built bus for Welcome of Newcastle. Behind is the original and smaller MCW-built version in service with Northumbria.
Stewart J. Brown

Delta single-decker in May 1988, and first displayed it at the NEC Show of that year. It marked the beginning of a relationship with the Dutch chassis manufacturer DAF Bus which was later to become much closer. The Delta was offered exclusively on the newly introduced DAF SB220 rear-engined bus chassis. and until the introduction of the Ikarus Citybus in 1991, the SB220 was offered only with the Delta body. As has continued to be the case, the extensive marketing campaign which supported Optare's sales stressed the Optare name rather than that of the chassis manufacturer.

Delta was the first Optare bus to employ the Alusuisse construction method involving the use of aluminium extrusions supplied by the Swiss licensee of the system. These extrusions are bolted together to form the structure which is completely corrosion-free. A great deal was made of the ease with which Delta could be repaired because all of the lower panels unbolted and the bumpers were in three sections. Ease of replacement was also the reason why gasket mounting rather than bonding was chosen for fixing the windows, though the one-piece roof panel was bonded to the main structure.

A part of the marketing strategy has always been the availability of demonstration vehicles from both Optare and the chassis manufacturer partner; the Delta was no exception to this. Soon these demonstration vehicles were touring the country and getting a very positive response. The magazine Commercial Motor borrowed one and Noel Millier commented, 'To describe the arrival of the Delta on the single-deck bus scene as 'significant' would be an understatement. For the stylish Optare bus has the potential to have an even greater effect on the single-deck bus market that its smaller, VW based brother, the City Pacer, had on the minibus scene — and that's saying something.'

When the UK Coach Rally was held at Southampton, a Bus of the Year award was presented annually. The Delta won it in 1989 and 1990, and, to complete a clean sweep, the Vecta took it the following year.

The first into revenue-earning service with an operator was delivered to Wigmore's of Dinnington, now Northern Bus, although this vehicle is now one of 10 with Walls of Manchester. To date, the biggest customers for the model have been Trent/Barton with

Top:
A sectioned MetroRider features in the bus exhibits at the London Transport Museum.
Stuart Jones

Bottom:
Cambus has bought both of Optare's main small bus models, the CityPacer and the MetroRider. This is a MetroRider.
Stewart J. Brown

54, many of which are used on that company's Rainbow routes, British Airways which bought 45 three-doorway examples, London Buses with its DA class of 34 buses including both single and dual-door models, Blackpool Transport with 28 plus three acquired with the Fylde business, Go-Ahead Group with 25, North East Bus with 22, Northumbria with 17, Reading Transport with 10 and PMT with nine. The Delta has proved very popular at airports where APCOA, Ralphs, Whytes, BAA (Gatwick), BCP and Capital have all bought examples in addition to the British Airways vehicles. The Ralphs buses have centre stepwell lifts while the five vehicles supplied to Ipswich Buses are unique in having a second doorway immediately behind the front axle; two of them being further distinguished by the choice of Voith transmissions rather than the standard ZF. Traditional independent purchasers include Marchwood Motorways, Richards Bros, Ogdens, Seamarks, OK Travel and West's of Woodford Green. To date, around 350 have been delivered, although sales have slowed considerably in recent years.

MetroRider

Possibly spurred by the success of the City Pacer, MCW had hurriedly developed its 25-seat MetroRider in time to introduce the integral design at the 1986 NEC show, adding a stretched 33-seat version the following year. Over 1,000 were sold but with MCW losing money heavily, the Laird group decided to sell the company. The design rights and jigs for the MetroRider were acquired by Optare, and, together with DAF, the company subsequently also purchased the Metrobus and Metroliner designs.

As acquired, the MetroRider was not without its faults and Optare set about 'Optarising' the minibus, unveiling the first example at Coach & Bus '89 in the colours of Ipswich. The Cummins B series engine and Allison AT545 automatic transmission was retained. It also featured a stronger structure, new door and emergency door, new skirt panels, gasket glazing

and aluminium side panels among other changes, rapidly becoming Optare's most popular product to date. As it was a full integral design, there were also benefits for the company from the supply of parts.

Once again London Buses was a major customer with several subsidiaries benefiting from the type which it designated MRL. Other major customers included the Welsh municipalities of Cardiff and Newport, West Riding, Wilts & Dorset, City of Oxford, SMT, Go-Ahead Group, North East Bus,

Reading Transport, Northumbria, Kentish Bus, Cambus, Welcome and Capital Citybus. Among those taking smaller numbers were Black Prince, Reliance of Great Gonerby, ABC Travel and Heatons, and for the municipalities of Lancaster and Darlington, what turned out to be their last new purchases. Out-of-the-ordinary vehicles included four electrically-powered examples running in Southern Electric colours as part of the City of Oxford fleet and the very last pre-evolved MetroRider, a completely built up vehicle cut off diagonally from behind the driver to behind the passenger door. This sectioned bus appears out of a wall on the upper floor of the new London Transport Museum at Covent Garden. This is the museum's second Optare; it also has one of the original batch of Selkent Roundabout City Pacers.

In 1993 the MetroRider was completely revamped and a new version brought out which was dubbed the 'Evolved MetroRider'. The first example, one of a batch for West Riding, appeared at Coach & Bus '93. Features included an uprated Euro 1 version of the Cummins 6BT engine producing 130bhp which coupled with a GVW increased to 8,400kg enabled an additional five passengers to be carried. To the existing 8.4 and 7.0m models was added a 7.7m model, and there was a choice of 2.2 and 2.38m widths on the two lengthier options. A host of differences were incorporated of which the most noticeable were a restyled front, larger destination display, wider door, an uprated braking system, increased interior headroom, modular lights and a repositioned rear destination display. I drove the 8.4m demonstrator for a day and found it one of the most pleasant minibuses I have ever driven.

Other customers for 'Evolved MetroRiders' include Nottingham City Transport, Lowland, East Surrey, PMT, Lincolnshire Roadcar, London & Country and Pennine Blue.

United Bus

In the process of developing and marketing the Delta, Optare had built up a good relationship with DAF Bus. When, late in 1989 the chassis manufacturer joined forces with the Dutch integral coach builder — Bova, to form United Bus — Optare followed suit and joined in the summer of 1990. Den Oudsten of the Netherlands and DAB Silkeborg of Denmark further expanded the group in the same year.

The United Bus philosophy was that by working closely together, each group member would gain access to more markets, achieve savings on design and development costs as well as benefiting from greater purchasing strength, and become a stronger player in the increasingly competitive market. In practice, there was a failure to rationalise, resulting in a duplication of many functions. Worse, the European bus market, particularly the Dutch market, dropped very dramatically. While most members were hit, Den Oudsten was devastated by the downturn and considerable investment was put into developing new products which it would be able to sell in a wider market.

The problems proved insurmountable for the young United Bus and it collapsed in late 1993. Surprisingly all of its constituents survived. For Russell Richardson it meant a battle to put together a management buyout plan in the face of competing bids. Eventually this was accomplished and the company returned to independence in December 1993.

Vecta

During its membership of United Bus, Optare had continued to develop and launch new products, the first of which was the 10m Vecta single-decker bus, exclusively available on the air suspended MAN 11.190 chassis. Similar in appearance to the Delta but with a more upright front profile, the Vecta was also built using the Alusuisse system. Unlike earlier Optare products sales were slow to take off and at the time of writing remained under the 100 mark. The lion's share went to the North East Bus group and its predecessors which took 52 prior to its acquisition by West Midlands Travel. Reading took batches of five and three, Trent bought 12 and Crosville Wales acquired a quartet in December 1994. Seamarks purchased several former demonstrators, Hutchinsons of Overtown bought three and should by now have taken delivery of a further pair, and Stevensons, West Coast Motors and Richards Brothers had all acquired single examples at the time of going to press. Black Prince of Morley took four early in 1995.

Spectra

Membership of United Bus was not an entirely bad experience for Optare. One of the positive things to come out of the alliance was the double-deck Spectra. Mounted on the DAF DB250 chassis it was the sensation of Coach & Bus '91 when it made its début in Reading livery. Apart from the driveline configuration, rear axle and rear air suspension system, the design owed very little to the Metrobus, and rather more to the SB220. The vertical DAF RS200 8.65 litre engine was mounted transversely at the rear and a choice of ZF or Voith automatic gearbox options was offered. Height options of 4.32 and 4.17m were offered for the 10.2m long vehicle, and a maximum capacity of 81 was advertised for single door versions.

Reading followed the launch of Spectra with additional orders including two coach specification versions for London express services. London Buses bought 24, most of them single door versions for London Central. Stevensons bought a pair and East Yorkshire one, but by far the most enthusiastic UK customer has been Wilts & Dorset which had taken delivery of 36 by the end of 1994. An unpainted Spectra with no interior which served as a test vehicle can still be found at the DAF Bus International plant at Eindhoven.

Following Optare's lead, both Alexander with its Royale and Northern Counties with the Palatine II, brought more stylish double-deck designs to the market.

Sigma

In the spring of 1994 Optare held a press conference at Covent Garden to show the first example of its new Sigma on the Dennis Lance underframe. The first Crossgates product to be mounted on a Dennis chassis since the initial batch of Dominos, the Sigma married the more upright front of the Vecta with the Delta structure. Ipswich took the first example and this was followed by 14 for Go-Ahead Northern, two for Trent and one for Busways. Later in 1994 it was announced that Optare would also body the Mercedes Benz O405 with a design that would incorporate the standard Mercedes front panel. The GRT Bus group announced a large order for the model, which was launched as the Prisma.

Also on display alongside the Sigma was a Bova Futura Express, part of the Bova range for which Optare has assumed importership responsibility through its Bova UK subsidiary. Working closely with long standing Bova dealer, the Moseley group, Bova UK has increased sales of the model in Britain.

Exports

From the early stages of Optare's development there has been an awareness of the possibilities offered by export markets. A deal with the Dutch minibus dealership CAB saw it offering left-hand drive City

Above:
Among the more unusual MetroRiders were those built to operate on battery power in Oxford. There were four — but each weighed almost 2.5 tonnes more than a standard diesel-powered model.
Stewart J. Brown

Pacers and StarRiders from 1987, among customers being the NZH organisation. At least a dozen left-hand drive StarRiders have been built, several of which have been sold in Luxembourg. There have also been sales to Irish operators.

Ironically, given the current association between the companies, Bova had agreed to market MCW Metrorider coaches on the continent before Optare acquired the design. Unfortunately quality standards greatly disappointed the Dutch importers and the agreement was short-lived. The 'Optarised' MetroRider has been a different proposition on the export market, and although the company has never offered coach versions, the MetroRider has been its most successful export model. Two were shipped to Norway, but the major breakthrough came with a CKD deal with the Malaysian company Diversified Resources Bhd. The agreement includes the transfer of manufacturing technology, the supply of CKD kits and after-sales support through Optare's Unitec service division. DRB's Intrakota Consolidated subsidiary operates the vehicles which are known in Malaysia as 'PekanRiders' (or PeopleRiders).

No Deltas, Vectas or Sigmas have been exported though the Delta has been exhibited at a number of European shows, and the Spectra double-decker has proved popular in Turkey where IETT Istanbul and Izulas of Izmir have taken batches of dual door vehicles.

The Future

The pace of change in the industry makes predictions about the future difficult, especially in an article written almost a year before most people will read it. A change of government policy towards positive support for public transport could make a significant difference to Optare and other manufacturers, but there is little sign of it yet.

There is no doubt that British operators appreciate the stylishness of Optare's vehicles and the durability of the Alusuisse construction system, but with a decreasing number of players as big groups with standardised buying policies gain an ever larger slice of the operating market, it becomes increasingly difficult to win orders.

Optare is better placed for survival than some of its smaller competitors because it has a modern product range covering all market sectors, a reputation for quality, and its products are more likely to appeal to overseas markets than some more traditionally British designs. It would be nice to see Optare-bodied Mercedes O405s on the export figures as well as the import figures.

Innovation has enabled the company to survive 10 of the most difficult years the bus and coach industry has witnessed. I have been impressed continually by what has been achieved and look forward to seeing what else Russell Richardson and his team have in store.

RE: Reliable Engineering

The Bristol RE was the most successful of the first-generation rear-engined single-deckers. **Tim Carter** pays tribute to one operator's REs, looking at the Hartlepool fleet shortly before it was acquired by Stagecoach.

Many regarded the Bristol RE as a classic bus design and since it was first announced in July 1962 it has had many supporters. Several members of the National Bus Company built up large fleets before the arrival of the all-conquering Leyland National. The largest RE operators were United Auto and Bristol Omnibus with deliveries of 470 and 425 respectively.

Sales to British operators ceased in 1975 and in most fleets the RE has either gone, or is reduced to a few soldiering on with their days numbered. Having said that, new supporters of the model have entered the scene, the most notable being the Northern Bus Co of Sheffield which has built up a sizeable fleet, including some brought back to England from Northern Ireland. Busways Travel Services in Newcastle has also been

buying second-hand REs in not insignificant numbers.

So old operators have been phasing them out, while new converts have been phasing them in. But while these changes have been taking place, one operator has stayed loyal to the RE since it took its first example back in 1967. That operator is Hartlepool Borough Transport, which — at the time of writing in a fast-changing world — still operates a fleet of REs which it has owned since new.

Hartlepool's decision to switch from crew-operated double-deckers to one-person-operated single-deckers coincided with the relaxation of sales restrictions on Bristol chassis and Eastern Coach Works bodies, following the acquisition of a share in both companies by Leyland. The last double-deckers for the Hartlepool fleet were two Roe-bodied Titans in 1965; all subsequent purchases were single-decked.

Some of the fleet's earliest opo single-deckers reflected part of this relaxation, being Leyland Leopard L1 chassis with ECW dual-door 42-seat bodies featuring wrap-round windscreens of the style fitted to bodywork being supplied on contemporary REs. They had D-suffix registrations and were the first ECW-bodies to be supplied to an operator outside the state-owned groups since nationalisation almost 20 years earlier.

Below:
This 1970 bus was one of the oldest REs in use when Hartlepool sold out to Stagecoach in 1994.
ALL PHOTOGRAPHS BY THE AUTHOR

Above:
The dual-purpose RE, rebuilt to single-doorway layout, received a coach-like livery of cream with maroon and yellow relief and bold Hartlepool Transport fleetnames.

The following year seven more vehicles were delivered. Once again they had two-door ECW bodies, but this time with 48 seats (and room for 23 standing) on Leyland-engined Bristol RELL6L chassis. The bodies differed visually from those on the Leopards, in that ECW had now developed a new front-end design with shallow flat-glass windscreens. They were less attractive, but cut windscreen replacement costs. These buses, Nos 39-45, were to be the first step in a long association with ECW-bodied RELLs. No-one could have foreseen that 25 years later, broadly similar buses would still be giving all-day service to the citizens of Hartlepool.

A further six identical buses, Nos 46-51, followed in 1968. Deliveries for 1969 were seven more RELL6Ls, Nos 52-58, but ECW had now revised the frontal appearance of its standard single-deck body once again, this time by fitting a deeper flat windscreen. This improved visibility and also made the bodies look better but it didn't address the problem of internal reflections, which could make night driving difficult. This was the only batch of Hartlepool REs to have deep flat screens. All future REs would feature the BET-style double curvature screen which was adopted as standard by ECW right across its range of bodies — and would remain the standard until the company's closure in the mid-1980s.

During the early 1970s several other types of bus were inspected by Hartlepool. These included two Metro-Scanias, a Seddon Pennine RU and a Tyneside Passenger Transport Executive Bristol RESL6L. None of these convinced Hartlepool to change from the reliable RELL/ECW combination.

Between 1970 and 1975 no fewer than 37 more ECW-bodied RELL6Ls joined the fleet, with deliveries continuing as long as the chassis was available to home-market buyers. The final batch, which took the fleet number series up to 96, were among the last REs to enter service in England, and they had the highest chassis numbers too. Hartlepool now ran 57 REs in a fleet which was 91 buses strong.

All but one of the 1970s REs were built as 46-seat buses. The odd man out was No 91, the last bus in the penultimate order, which had 42 dual-purpose seats (but still in a two-door body) to make it suitable for private hire. It was later rebuilt as a 47-seater with the centre exit door being removed. Another noteworthy feature was that it was the last bus to carry a Hartlepool EF-series registration, GEF191N. Reorganisation of the vehicle registration offices in 1974 meant that Hartlepool no longer issued its own marks and the last REs carried former North Riding AJ-series registrations.

By the early 1990s, the surviving REs were still hard at work, having outlasted some later types, most notably single-deck Dennis Dominators.

During a visit to the town in August 1993 examples of every batch of curved-windscreen RE could be seen in service including No 59, the first of the type. Some, it has to be said, looked ready for a coat of paint, but despite their age they didn't look out of place, even alongside new L-registered Optare Deltas in the United fleet. Which raised two questions: would Deltas still be running with United when they were 23 years old, and just how much longer could Hartlepool's REs last?

Left:
One of the last batch, delivered in 1975, still in all-day service 18 years later.

Below:
The end in sight? The ECW body on the RE had a distinctive rear end with its centrally-positioned emergency exit.

The answer to the first question will take some time to manifest itself. A partial answer to the second came in November 1994, when Hartlepool Borough Transport was bought by Stagecoach Holdings.

When Stagecoach took over Hartlepool was running 65 buses and six coaches. Over half of the buses — 35 in all — were REs, the oldest being H-registered examples, now in their 24th year. Stagecoach has maintained a high level of investment in new buses and it would seem to be just a matter of time before operation of REs in Hartlepool becomes just a memory.

Hartlepool's Bristol REs

Fleet No	Registration	New
39-45	FEF39-45E	1967
46-51	HEF46-51F	1968
52-58	JEF652-658G	1969
59-65	LEF59-65H	1970
66-72	MEF66-72J	1971
73-79	OEF73-79K	1972
80-84	SEF80-84L	1973
85-91	GEF185-191N	1975
92-95	JAJ292-295N	1975

Taken over by Stagecoach in 1994: Nos 59-61, 64-67, 69-96

Bright green Jersey

No, the bright green jersey was not an item of **Malcolm Keeley's** wardrobe in the swinging 1960s. It was, he recalls, an island holiday destination...

It was the summer of 1968, the time when the forces of youthful freedom that had been building up throughout the decade finally took on the establishment in a bid for worldwide revolution and a new era.

I wasn't conscious of being in the vanguard of this global revolution, but I can now see I was. My part, armed only with a fine calibre girlfriend, was to take on... the seaside landlady. Just like my more overt partners in the struggle, I fought the law and the law won, but subsequent improvements in bed and breakfast accommodation are undoubtedly due in no small way to my inadvertent campaign of guerilla warfare waged in 1968.

The chosen battlefield was St Helier, Jersey, long before the days of middle-aged detectives capering about in unsuitable sports cars that would have been retired even in 1968. Mind you, Jersey was still a place for oldish motors although not as elderly as only a few years previously. The early 1960s had seen a modernisation that had swept away an incredible range of late 1920s and 1930s buses, mostly Leylands, many returning to the mainland and their former guises to form the nucleus of the preservation movement. There was still much to see, nevertheless.

Below:
The oldest operational vehicle in the JMT fleet in 1968 was this 1946 Mulliner-bodied Bedford OB, the last survivor of the Safety Coach Service fleet, absorbed in 1946.
ALL PHOTOGRAPHS BY THE AUTHOR

Top:
A 1947 Leyland Tiger PS1 with 34-seat bodywork by Wallace Arnold subsidiary Wilks & Meade climbs over Mount Bingham with Queen Elizabeth castle and St. Helier harbour as a backdrop.

Middle:
The second of the hairpin bends on Mount Bingham is successfully negotiated by a 1947 all-Leyland Titan.

Bottom:
Looking considerably older than its years, a 1949 Reading-bodied Dennis Pax ia caught at Greve de Lecq. It was a 21-seater.

Top right:
Mulliner bodies were fitted to a batch of Albion Victors delivered in 1949.

Below right:
The Cafe Miranda would seem to have much to commend it with its splendid view of the Weighbridge. Each JMT service had its own space painted on the bus station with a further area reserved for buses not required for immediate service, such as this Reading-bodied Dennis Falcon and Mulliner-bodied Albion Victor.

Jersey is much closer geographically to France than to Great Britain and its administration is independent of Whitehall. The much lower levels of taxation were astonishing even then with cigarettes at two shillings (10p) for 20 and petrol at 3/6 (17.5p) a gallon. Firstly one had to get there and, with cheap air fares not yet around the corner, this meant a stomach-churning crossing by boat. The attractive blonde lady handing out 'What's on in Jersey' booklets to new arrivals hastened recovery, however, and was in stark contrast to the grim-faced line of

customs officers awaiting the happy holidaymakers landing at Weymouth.

St Helier's Weighbridge bus station was just a stone's throw away from the quay. Several sightings of the immaculately restored Leyland TD2 J6332 of Michael Banfield at Brighton rallies had prepared me for the delightful apple green and cream buses of Jersey Motor Transport, so reminiscent of one of my favourite bus companies, Southdown, now Stagecoached out of existence. Since the closure of a remarkable bus station in a former railway cutting, complete with a turntable to turn buses around in the

restricted space, all services either terminated or passed through the Weighbridge and thus the entire fleet could be viewed there at one time or another.

The entire early postwar fleet of Leyland PD1 and PD2 Titans with Leyland's own highbridge bodies could still be found; indeed one of the trio of PD1s had just been beautifully repainted despite its 21 years of age. Greater variety came with the regrettable cessation of body construction at Leyland. The year 1955 saw a pair of PD2s with the then ubiquitous Metro-Cammell Orion bodies and these were followed by five with relatively rare Reading bodies; the 1958

Top left:
This 1951 Tiger PS1 had Reading bodywork. It later moved to Guernsey and achieved a new lease of life as an open-topper.

Middle left:
One of the last of the classic Leyland-bodied buses was this 1954 PD2/10 seen at the Weighbridge. A combined island tour and rover ticket cost a hefty 37s 6d (£1.87).

Bottom left:
JMT's newest double-deckers were 1958 PD2s with concealed radiators and rare double-deck bodywork by Reading.

batch being of five-bay construction and the 1959 four-bay. The real 'modernisation' had been achieved subsequent to these, however, with a considerable number of ex-London Transport RTLs, which looked uneasy with their 'J' registrations. These worked the basic 15min headway on trunk route 1 (Gorey-St Helier-St Aubin), assisted by other Titans as duplicates.

The single-deck fleet was equally absorbing, the oldest being a 1946 Bedford OB with Mulliner bus body which was the last survivor of the Safety Coach Service fleet. Next in seniority was a pair of 1946 Leyland PS1 Tigers with rare Wilkes & Meade bodies. One remained in original rear-entrance form and looked remarkably vintage but the other had been facelifted by Reading; this work included the relocation of the entrance to the front. Two further PS1s were in stock — late models dating from circa

1951. These had smart pay-as-you-enter bodies, but have since gone on to greater fame as open-toppers on sister island Guernsey.

Albion Victors formed the bulk of the single-deck stock. Particular favourites were the late 1940s examples with Mulliner bodies, but the majority, delivered between 1953 and 1958, had Reading bodies. Forward-control Dennis Falcons, looking like fire engines with Reading bus bodies, bridged the gap in 1951/52. Pride of place went to the porcine pair of Reading-bodied Dennis Pax which, despite dating from 1949, resembled the far more numerous Ace models of prewar years. Later series comprised 10 Massey-bodied Leyland Tiger Cubs, including short length examples for the restricted roads, whilst four Albion Vikings with Pennine Coachcraft bodies were only a year old.

The St Helier town service had been virtually restocked with Bedford VAS1s followed in 1968 by Seddon Pennine IVs, all with Pennine Coachcraft bodies. A miniature Dennis Triton/Reading of 1953 and an ex-Joes Bus Service 1958 Morris Commercial/Thurgood, however, still survived to battle through the narrow congested streets.

The first task, however, was to locate the booked bed and breakfast house on Havre des Pas. This was a 4d bus ride from the Weighbridge, which turned out to be excellent value for the enthusiast as Mount Bingham had to be tackled. This comprised two hairpin bends, a stiff climb followed by a bottleneck on a rather nasty downward gradient. This lot had to be tackled by all eastbound buses, including double-deckers on route 1. I understand all this entertainment has now been replaced by a tunnel.

The B&B was welcoming enough, but the landlady explained that we were the first guests since her road accident and she was still feeling below par. It was, therefore, unfortunate that my first wash led to the basin plug becoming jammed. A hearty pull separated the chain, leaving the plug lurking sulkily in its hole, which it refused to leave, despite every encouragement from myself, the girlfriend and, finally, the landlady. 'Twas on the Monday morning the plumber came to call.

Monday was not a good day generally as we discovered when we endeavoured to shelter from the rain in the B&B.

'You can't come back in here during the day. What do you think this is? An hotel?'

The weather subsequently improved and time was spent on the beach — skin cancer and premature skin ageing had not been invented then. This too ended in disaster as we failed to spot the local oil slick as we padded off the sand.

'What are all these stains on the staircarpet?' came the cry as the landlady tracked all too easily the trail of black footprints leading guiltily to our rooms. Note 'rooms' plural; the summer of love did not extend to Jersey as I discovered when the landlady ordered me

out of the girlfriend's room whilst I was innocently in there in search of a 10 bob note!

Never mind, there was still the all-day round-the-island tour to enjoy. Several coach operators offered such trips, with petrol-engined Bedfords being the norm. JMT's immaculate buses were ruined by ghastly luminous pink advertisements, including those of its coaching subsidiary Rover Tours. We succumbed to this un-Jerseylike high-pressure selling although, being poverty stricken, we rejected the posh tour, priced at just under a pound which included hostess-served meals, in favour of the 12/6 (62.5p) tour which did not include nosh.

We were allocated to a newish (1964) Bedford SB3, astonishingly petrol-powered, with rare Strachans body. This was pleasing as most of the Rover Tours fleet was Duple-bodied, including a smart 1948 OB which displayed itself at various strategic points on the Weighbridge although I never saw it actually move. Perhaps it was reserved for 'Krazy' nights where passengers apparently provided the entertainment by getting thoroughly inebriated and dressing up as members of the opposite sex, etc. Depressingly typical in these decadent times but definitely suspect then!

The tour covered every bay and item of interest, including excursions down roads positively made-to-measure. No obstacle proved too much for our driver, who also treated us to a lengthy lecture on the two types of tomato found on the island. Between tomato talks he protested about new-fangled ideas like traffic lights — poor blighter had no idea what was to come.

The lunch break was taken at Greve de Lecq, where one of the antediluvian Dennis Pax buses was an unexpected delicacy. The teatime stop was made at Gorey where I failed to duplicate the fine photo in Buses Illustrated 134 showing a bus on service 1 with the impressive Mont Orgueil castle as a backdrop.

The weather deteriorated as the first week drew to a close. The beleaguered landlady was suffering from increasing wear and tear and muttered that she had reopened to guests (there was only us!) before her recovery was complete. Perhaps it was the evidence of further disasters around the premises: the perforation where the doorknob had burst through the new wallpaper to reveal a cavity rather than plaster; the tell-tale signs of my unforgivable attempt to emulate movie heroes by removing a bottletop through sharp impact on the corner of a stout object such as a bedframe — forgetting, of course, that Bogart and company did not drink fizzy cola and got it right first time, thus sparing themselves the eventual cascade of Pepsi to the ceiling, falling as gentle rain on to the counterpane.

The undeclared war between inexperienced youth and tired establishment thus moved into the negotiation stage and Mrs B&B explained that, once it started raining in Jersey, it never stopped. Going home early seemed a good idea, although it meant I barely

Top:
JMT bought ex-London Transport RTLs to update its fleet. Former RTL485 edges its way through the narrow approach to Havre des Pas, St Helier, pursued by a Massey-bodied Tiger Cub.

Above:
Rover Tours, a JMT subsidiary, ran three unusual Strachans-bodied Bedford SB3s. These dated from 1964 and had petrol engines. Fleet numbers were applied in words: Rover Three pauses at Bouley Bay.

got beyond black-and-white photographs and into the colour slide film. A week in Perranporth with (and, therefore, heavily subsidised by) the future in-laws beckoned in lieu, together with rebodied Bristol L types and cream semi-coach Lodekkas, and somewhere to go when it rained.

Comeback

In the 1970s, Bristol's VRT fell from favour in Scotland and most of those in the country were sold south of the border. But in recent years the VRT has made a Scottish comeback, as **Billy Nicol** illustrates.

Overleaf top:
Former Scottish Bus Group subsidiary Lowland Omnibuses bought this ECW-bodied VRT from Southern Vectis in 1990 and rebuilt it with a standard SBG-style triangular destination display.
ALL PHOTOGRAPHS BY THE AUTHOR

Overleaf bottom:
Kelvin Central Buses acquired VRTs from a number of sources. This former Bristol Omnibus vehicle is seen in central Glasgow in 1993. Its stay with KCB was brief.

Opposite top:
Just over 20 VRTs were transferred to the Fife Scottish fleet in 1994 from other Stagecoach subsidiaries. The farthest travelled and most unusual were four Willowbrook-bodied buses from Stagecoach South's East Kent operation. Two are seen in Cowdenbeath depot.

Opposite bottom:
Ready for attention on the steam-cleaning ramp is a one-time Cumberland VRT in the fleet of Rennies of Dunfermline. It is one of three purchased from Bluebird Northern in 1993.

Above:
Moffat & Williamson of Gauldry built up a network of local services in Fife, and at one stage was running 20 VRTs, including two ex-Thames Transit buses. One pulls out of Glenrothes bus station in the spring of 1994 shortly before Moffat & Williamson gave up the bulk of its local bus operation.

National HERITAGE

Remember the National Bus Company? Its privatisation started 10 years ago.
Stewart J. Brown looks back.

Enthusiasts had bewailed the onset of NBC's new corporate colours when they were announced in 1972. The brash red and drab green, and the standardised block-letter fleetnames which came with them, ousted years of tradition. Vehicle standardisation soon followed, and by the end of the decade NBC companies were largely taking Leyland Nationals and ECW-bodied Bristol VRTs, with a sprinkling of Park Royal/Roe-bodied Atlanteans for the non-conformists.

Bristol LHs were delivered in small numbers for rural routes. Coaches — in unrelieved white which often looked shabby — were mainly Leopards bodied by Britain's two big coach builders, Duple and Plaxton.

The National Bus Company's proud boast in the 1970s was that it was the world's biggest bus and coach operator. At its peak its fleet numbered over 20,000 vehicles. For much of the 1970s and into the early 1980s its two standard liveries, poppy red or leaf green depending on which part of the country you lived in, could be seen if not from Land's End to John' o Groats, certainly from Land's End to Berwick-on-Tweed. It seems hard to believe that, for example, buses in Canterbury could be the same colour as buses in Carlisle — but they were. Though, come to think of it, maybe nothing much has changed…

It was hardly an exciting time. But as the 1980s progressed, the Conservative Government pursued the privatisation of nationalised industries with zeal. In 1985 it was announced that NBC was to be privatised. Its top management lobbied for privatisation as a single unit — but, responded the Government, that would have conflicted with yet another Great Conservative Cause: local bus deregulation and competition.

Deregulation was designed to encourage new, small, entrepreneurs. The existence of an operation as big as NBC would militate against competition.

Left:
The old order: a Southern National Bristol RE in corporate NBC colours. New in 1968, this RE was long-lived. It is seen in Minehead in 1985.
ALL PHOTOGRAPHS BY STEWART J. BROWN

Above:
Before being bought by Stagecoach, Ribble had modified the NBC poppy red scheme by adding grey and yellow relief. The end result was attractive, as shown by a one-time Midland Red Fleetline, part of a large fleet of second-hand buses acquired by Ribble for post-deregulation expansion.

Indeed, such was the Government's anxiety — nay, paranoia — about big companies stifling competition that it instructed that some of NBC's biggest subsidiaries be split up.

Thus were born such varied operations as Northumbria Motor Services, North Western, Milton Keynes City Bus, Luton & District, Brighton & Hove, Badgerline, Crosville Wales, the imaginatively titled Alder Valley North and South companies (no big consultancy fees for new names and liveries here) and the four parts of London Country Bus Services. Other companies, notably Ribble and United had to split off parts of their operations to their neighbours, Cumberland and East Yorkshire respectively.

To further encourage competition and discourage new monopolistic companies from emerging, no one bidder for an NBC operation was allowed to takeover ownership of more than three companies. And the three companies had to be geographically separate. Nice plan, shame it didn't work.

1986: the first sales

The first sale, in July 1986, was of National Holidays. It went to Pleasurama, owners of Smiths Happiways Shearings, and underpinned the company's position as Britain's biggest coach tour operator. National Holidays owned no coaches; these were generally hired in from other NBC companies.

The first bus business to be sold was Devon General, bought by its management in August — and 10 years on, still management-owned. Which marks a relatively rare case of stable ownership of an NBC management buyout (MBO). Many other MBOs saw periods of rapid changes in ownership as the buyout teams decided their money would be better invested in a building society than in a bus company.

In fact all of the sales in the autumn and winter of 1986 were to MBOs — Devon General was followed by Badgerline, Southern Vectis, Cheltenham & Gloucester, Maidstone & District, Cambus, PMT, South Midland, Midland Red West (with Midland Red Coaches), Eastern National and Trent. It would have been a brave man who would have dared forecast that one of the 11 names in that list would 10 years later own four of the others. And that it would be named after a nocturnal flea-ridden animal.

South Midland had a short life. In the spring of 1987 Devon General set up a minibus operation in Oxford, Thames Transit, competing head-on with City of Oxford Motor Services. It followed this up by buying South Midland in the summer, and ultimately absorbed the South Midland business at the end of 1988. Thames Transit also competed with City of

Top left:
Midland Red West was for a short time owned by its management. It later became part of Badgerline.

Middle left:
South Midland was short-lived. It was formed in 1984, taking over part of City of Oxford's business, was privatised in 1986 and was absorbed by Transit Holdings at the end of 1988. For a short period its fleet included ex-Greater Manchester Leyland Titans. One is seen in Oxford in the summer of 1988.

Bottom left:
Crosville switched from NBC leaf green to a bizarre combination of dark green and orange, before substituting cream for the orange to produce a smart, if conservative, livery. The company was briefly owned by ATL (Western) before being purchased by Drawlane and split up.

Top right:
The new livery adopted by the Berks Bucks Bus company — Alder Valley North as was — featured yellow with a minimum of dark grey relief. The only new double-deckers bought by the privatised company have been five Leyland Olympians with Northern Counties bodies.

Below right:
Remember Hastings & District? It was a short-lived operation, created in 1983 to take over the Hastings operations of Maidstone & District, the original owners of this highbridge VRT. It was sold to its management in 1987, and to Stagecoach in 1989.

Oxford on its busy London City Link coach service, launching the imaginatively-titled Thames Tube.

1987: boom year for sales

The pattern of successful MBOs continued at the start of 1987 with City of Oxford, Yorkshire Traction, West Riding and the associated Yorkshire Woollen company; East Yorkshire, Eastern Counties and East Kent being sold to their respective management teams in the first three months of the year.

The first vehicle-owning company to go to an outside buyer was National Travel (East) which went to ATL Holdings, ATL being the initials of Tony Lavin, the man behind the company which also ran

Top:
East Kent was a successful management buyout — but eventually joined the growing Stagecoach empire on the south coast. A standard NBC-style VRT illustrates the livery used between NBC and Stagecoach ownership.

Middle:
East Midland adopted an attractive two-tone green livery, as illustrated by a Bristol VRT in Chesterfield, the company's home town. This livery was one of the many casualties of the advance of Stagecoach's corporate white scheme.

Bottom:
Badgerline's smart green and yellow livery on a Leyland National in Bath. The Badgerline group steered clear of corporate colours, but did apply the badger logo to buses in other group companies.

Top right:
Cheltenham & Gloucester, owners of this Leyland National 3, as the company styled its refurbished examples, expanded by taking over the neighbouring Red & White operation. But soon after it sold out to Stagecoach.

Middle right:
London Country South East was the first of the four London Country companies to shake off the old influences and adopt a fresh new image, as shown by this ex-London Country Atlantean in Woolwich.

Bottom right:
London Country North West originally retained NBC green but substituted a bright green relief band between decks in place of NBC's white, which improved the fleet's appearance more than might be imagined. An Atlantean in this interim livery is seen in Watford. The company later painted its buses grey and green.

Carlton PSV, the Rotherham-based Neoplan importer. Carlton/ATL had, since 1985, owned Yelloway Motor Services, the old-established Rochdale coach firm. Yelloway had a long and distinguished past; under ATL ownership it faced a short and unhappy future.

National Travel (East) was in quick succession renamed NTE Coaches and then SUT, and under the SUT banner started running local bus services in Sheffield, taking advantage of deregulation. Yelloway, incidentally, also started running local services in Greater Manchester. The SUT initials stood for Sheffield United Transport — but ATL was unable to spell that out because ownership of the full name lay with Wallace Arnold Tours.

The next operator to go to an outside bidder was Hampshire Bus, with the associated Pilgrim Coaches fleet, in April. The name Skipburn might not be a familiar one, but this was the buyer. It was in fact a holding company set up by Stagecoach, a small Perthshire-based coach operator which had started making waves in Perth and Glasgow, running ex-London Routemasters on local services in competition with established operators in both cities. In an indication of some of the complex wheeler-dealing which was to mark the next few years, Stagecoach quickly sold the Southampton area operations of Hampshire Bus to Southern Vectis (which had already established its own 20-strong Solent Blue Line operation in the city). But

Above:
Routemasters arrived at United Counties in advance of Stagecoach's decision to adopt a corporate livery. They entered service in United Counties green, but with Routemaster as the fleet name.

there was to be no Pilgrim's progress; the small coaching operation was closed down.

More MBOs followed in the early summer: National Welsh, Northern General, Brighton & Hove, South Wales Transport, Wilts & Dorset and Wessex National. Provincial was sold to an employee co-operative, with each of the company's employees having an equal stake.

A new name appeared for the next outside sale — Drawlane of Salisbury, which acquired Shamrock & Rambler Coaches in July. Drawlane was a subsidiary of Endless Holdings, which also owned Allied Bus Services. Despite its name, ABS was not an operator, and during the summer, confusion reigned about the Endless/Drawlane/Allied connection and their eligibility to buy more than three companies between them. Endless was named as the successful bidder for North Devon and Southern National, while Allied was to get Midland Red North, Lincolnshire Road Car and East Midland. All of these decisions were challenged — mainly by other bidders — and in the end only Midland Red North went to the Endless/Drawlane/Allied group.

In the second half of 1987 Stagecoach raised a few eyebrows by buying Cumberland and United Counties, bringing its combined fleet up to 800 buses by the year end, compared with around 100 just 12 months earlier.

It was remarkable growth by any standards for a company which was just five years old. No one could have foreseen that the expansion would continue…

Straightforward MBOs in the latter part of 1987 comprised Milton Keynes City Bus, Luton & District, Southdown, Northumbria, Hastings & District and Crosville Wales. Midland Fox of Leicester was a partial MBO, but with some involvement from Stevensons of Uttoxeter which took over the company's Swadlincote operations.

Badgerline, privatised in September 1986, first flexed its purchasing muscles in August 1987 when it joined forces with Plympton Coachlines of Plymouth to buy Western National. Badgerline during 1987 set up competitive services in Poole and Portsmouth through jointly-owned companies. In Poole it had linked up with Southern Vectis to form Badger Vectis, and in Portsmouth a link with local authority-owned Southampton City Transport saw the formation of Red Admiral. But the Western National purchase with Plympton Coachlines was its first acquisition; it would later assume sole ownership, after buying out Plympton's interests.

At West Yorkshire another new set of initials appeared: AJS. As at ATL, AJS were the initials of the man leading the purchase, Alan Stephenson, who was chairman of East Yorkshire. Stephenson was working with West Yorkshire's managers, so this was a partial MBO, but it differed from most in that the company's property was not part of the deal, being sold separately to Parkdale Holdings.

At Bristol Omnibus, trading as City Line, the

Frontsource. It had taken over NBC's eight separate engineering companies in March, and it moved from bus repair into bus operation in October with the acquisition of Alder Valley South, the Aldershot-based part of the former Alder Valley company.

Also new was Q Drive, set up by Len Wright, well known as an operator of high-specification coaches for pop group tours and since mid-1985 a bus operator running a London Regional Transport tendered route in Hounslow. In December 1987 Q Drive took over what had been Alder Valley North but had since January been the Berks Bucks Bus Co, more catchily known as The Bee Line.

There were odd flurries of activity during 1987. PMT, for example, established operations in Wirral and Leeds. East Yorkshire took over the Scarborough area bus operations of Wallace Arnold, and set up a Scarborough & District company. Luton & District acquired Red Rover of Aylesbury. Trent acquired a small shareholding in the Leicester City Bus business, its price for Leicester's withdrawal from Trent territory in Loughborough.

1988: the end of the beginning

The first of the four London Country companies to be sold, London Country North West, was the first sale of 1988. It was an MBO, as were East Midland, Ribble, National Express and the joint Southern National/North Devon sales which quickly followed.

After the hiatus of 1987, Drawlane (which owned only Shamrock & Rambler in Bournemouth) moved forward rapidly in 1988 taking over Midland Red North, London Country South West and North Western Road Car in just seven weeks between January and March. These three companies ran 975 buses between them.

Yorkshire Traction got Lincolnshire Road Car in January and ATL, last heard of at the start of 1987, bought Crosville in March through a new ATL (Western) subsidiary. Badgerline took over the National Travelworld chain of 86 travel agencies (selling them to Co-op Travel Care in 1989) and Frontsource added the one remaining engineering company, Gatwick Engineering, to its portfolio.

Kentish Bus, as London Country South East had become in the spring of 1987, was bought in March by Proudmutual, the holding company for Northumbria, followed by the last sale of all in April, when London Country North East went to AJS/Parkdale Holdings, the owners of West Yorkshire.

Victoria Coach Station was transferred to London Regional Transport on 1 April. It had taken 21 months to sell NBC's 72 subsidiaries, of which 59 were bus and coach operators. Of those 59, 36 had gone to

Above:
Britain's biggest bus group is Stagecoach, with most of its strength being built on ex-NBC operators such as Cumberland Motor Services, owners of this Alexander-bodied Olympian seen approaching Kendal on the lengthy route from Lancaster to Carlisle.

management had a minority stake in the purchase, with Midland Red West (privatised at the end of 1986) being the majority shareholder. Other previously-privatised NBC companies to expand by acquisition at the end of 1987 were Cheltenham & Gloucester, taking over the adjacent Midland Red South business; Eastern National, which acquired the small (six-vehicle) Voyage National business in Lille but quickly regretted it; and West Riding, which took over United Automobile Services. Both Cheltenham & Gloucester and West Riding effectively doubled the size of their businesses at a stroke.

New group names were appearing — Transit Holdings (running Devon General and Thames Transit), Western Travel (owning Cheltenham & Gloucester and Midland Red South) and Caldaire Holdings (owning West Riding, Yorkshire Woollen and United Auto). Caldaire also ran services in Sheffield through a new subsidiary, Sheffield & District, which it set up at the end of 1986 and sold to South Yorkshire Transport in 1989.

Another new — and short-lived — name was

Top:
Yorkshire Woollen and West Riding under Caldaire ownership have invested heavily in new buses. Recent deliveries have been Alexander Striders on Volvo B10B and, as seen here in Leeds, Dennis Lance chassis.

Middle:
London & Country, previously London Country South West, has made significant expansion into London. An East Lancs-bodied Volvo Citybus nears Trafalgar Square on one of the company's many LRT tendered services.

Bottom:
The Go-Ahead group has bought large numbers of Dennis Darts, most of which have bodies by Wright, as seen here, or Marshall. Northern is one of five main trading names used for the former Northern General companies.

Opposite:
A more original trading name used by the Go-Ahead group is VFM Buses, with the letters standing for value for money. An ECW-bodied Atlantean, purchased in NBC days, picks up passengers in South Shields.

management buyout teams. And that was that. Or was it? NBC had gone and a new order was established with a few small-to-medium-sized groups and a host of new-generation independent companies. Who could have foreseen the changes which were just around the corner…?

In 1988 Transit Holdings, well pleased with the success of its minibuses in Oxford, announced a new Basingstoke Transit operation to compete with Stagecoach's Hampshire Bus. Stagecoach responded with a free bus service in Torbay, in the heart of

Devon General territory and at the height of the summer season. There followed some behind-the-scenes action and at the last minute the Basingstoke Transit operation was abandoned before it started. Some of the buses earmarked for it were instead used to launch minibus services in London under the Docklands Transit banner in March 1989. This wasn't a success and folded after 18 months.

The prowling badger wasn't doing too well either in its first tentative forays into strange territory. Its Badger Vectis operation ceased suddenly in April 1988, under concerted attack from incumbent operator Wilts & Dorset, while in July it sold its share in Red Admiral of Portsmouth to Southampton City Bus, which now had a major stake in the established Portsmouth City Bus operation and obviously saw no sense in running two competing operations.

But where it was doing well was in takeovers. No sooner was the ink dry on the last NBC sale document than Badgerline announced the first major takeover of one former NBC company by another, when it acquired Midland Red West in April. The interesting feature of this was that it put Bristol Omnibus under Badgerline control, just over two years after the two operations had been divided to ensure that there was no one dominant operation in the Bristol area.

A toothless tiger, the Monopolies & Mergers Commission, was set on the badger's trail just in case the takeover proved to be anti-competitive. The MMC was to become a thorn in the industry's side. On the one hand the Government was espousing free-market

theories. On the other it was saying that the free market wasn't really that free after all, notably when it came to the sale of companies even where willing buyers were doing deals with willing sellers.

A few months after Badgerline and Bristol Omnibus were reunited in common ownership, the same happened at Alder Valley. It had been split in two at the start of 1986. In November 1988 Q Drive, owner of The Bee Line (previously Alder Valley North) bought Alder Valley South, ending just 12 months of bus operation by Frontsource.

An aggressively competitive operator turned out to be National Welsh. It was the first ex-NBC fleet to buy a municipal business when it took over Taff Ely's bus services in September 1987. This was followed in 1989 by Rhymney Valley — by then trading as Inter Valley Link. National Welsh's competitive tactics also played a major part in the closure of Merthyr Tydfil Transport in 1989.

The ATL group, with services in Leeds, Sheffield and Manchester, and ownership of Crosville, had evidently bitten off more than it could comfortably chew. During 1988 it had occasional trouble with the traffic commissioners over vehicle maintenance standards in some of its fleets and in November its Yelloway operation was taken over by Crosville.

After just six months in the private sector, National Express diversified into bus operation with the purchase of Crosville Wales from its MBO team. With a 470-strong fleet it was the first of the big MBO businesses to lose its independence — after less than

12 months.

Another early casualty was Voyage National, which Eastern National was trying to sell. National Express expressed interest but in the end decided not to go ahead and the French operation was put into receivership.

The process of amalgamation, as had happened with Badgerline in Bristol and with Q Drive in Alder Valley country, was but one side of the rapidly-changing bus business. Elsewhere, existing operations were being broken down into smaller units. In 1988 Caldaire hived off its Selby operations into a new Selby & District company, while AJS broke up the once-mighty West Yorkshire into three. It retained the West Yorkshire title for a 300-bus operation largely in what had been the West Yorkshire metropolitan county, and created York City & District with 120 buses and Harrogate & District with 70, each — at the risk of stating the obvious — serving the areas in their titles.

But the West Yorkshire operation was to see further change and in 1989 part was sold to Yorkshire Rider and the remainder re-formed as a new Keighley & District operation. West Yorkshire's coach fleet was sold to National Express and a new company, Yorkshire Voyager, formed to run it. In the south, AJS's London Country North East was set to disappear with the creation of two new companies, County Bus & Coach and Sovereign Bus & Coach. AJS added Premier Travel of Cambridge to its southern operations in February 1988, after takeover talks between Premier and Cambus fell through — but Cambus had only two years to wait before

retrenchment at AJS saw the sale of most of the Premier operation to the Cambridge-based group.

An inkling of new vehicle-buying policies for some of the ex-NBC companies emerged in 1988. The old NBC-Leyland links had been broken, but a fair number of the new companies stayed loyal to Leyland. Stagecoach, for example, standardised on Olympians, but Drawlane switched to Dennis, while Brighton & Hove went to Scania. Caldaire selected the Leyland Lynx as its new standard bus.

1989: the pace quickens

If anyone thought that the sale of NBC would create some new stability in the industry and encourage a new generation of small(ish) bus companies, 1989 showed that they were sadly mistaken.

Stagecoach started the year with its three original acquisitions, Hampshire Bus, Cumberland and United Counties; the maximum number it had been allowed to buy under the privatisation rules. But there was nothing in the rules to prevent subsequent purchases from the owners of companies who wanted to sell out. In quick succession Stagecoach bought three companies from their MBO teams — East Midland, Ribble and Southdown — and topped that off at the end of the year with Hastings & District. It had another operation in Hastings too, Top Line, set up in mid-1988 jointly by Southdown and Eastbourne Buses. Stagecoach had bought Eastbourne's share soon after the Southdown takeover.

Stagecoach's position in the Portsmouth area was consolidated with the purchase of Portsmouth City Bus in October, which was to be re-formed as

Left:
United, now owned by West Midlands Travel, still runs a number of Bristol LHs, NBC's standard light-duty bus. This LH was new to Bristol Omnibus in 1980. It reached United by way of Trimdon Motor Services.

Above:
Since privatisation Yorkshire Traction has been buying Scanias for its full-size buses. An Alexander-bodied N113 is seen in the centre of Rotherham.

Southdown Portsmouth. However here the MMC and the Department of Trade & Industry waded in, and in early 1991 the former Portsmouth business was sold to Transit Holdings and converted from ageing double-deckers to modern minibuses. Coincidentally Transit Holdings just happened to have a fleet of minibuses going spare following the closure of its Docklands Transit operation in London.

The Ribble takeover gave Stagecoach a strong presence in the northwest of England, and there was some redrawing of the Cumberland/Ribble boundary with over 100 buses going from Ribble to Cumberland. East Midland ran 30 buses on LRT tendered services and this operation, Frontrunner South East, was sold to Ensign Bus. Services in Essex which were operated by Frontrunner went to AJS's County Bus & Coach.

There was rationalisation in the northwest too, with Ribble taking over routes operated in Blackburn by Drawlane's North Western subsidiary, while Drawlane took over Stagecoach operations in Manchester which consisted of some Ribble routes, the former United Transport Bee Line Buzz which had been acquired with Ribble, and East Midland's Frontrunner North West operations.

Stagecoach was reported to be about to buy Milton Keynes City Bus at the end of 1989, but didn't. In fact MKCB survived in its original ownership until the end of 1992, when it was taken over by Cambus.

During 1989 Stagecoach also gave up its original express coach business, selling this to National Express, which set up Caledonian Express as a new brand name to replace Stagecoach. The net result of all these manoeuvres was that the Stagecoach group trebled in size in just 12 months, from 800 buses at the start of 1989 to 2,400 at the end. And there was more to come.

National Express was expanding in other directions too. The short-lived Thandi Express business, running 10 Yugoslavian-built TAZ Dubravas, lasted but six months in 1989. London Express was launched in April 1989 to provide feeder services on 19 routes to Victoria Coach Station; it quietly disappeared the following year. Joint venture coach businesses were set up — Durham Travel Services, Dorset Travel Services, Rotherham Travel Services, Trathens Travel Services, Tayside Travel Services and Yorkshire Voyager Travel Services. In each case these companies provided coaches in National Express livery for use on express services. The Durham and Dorset companies had previously been the coaching operations of United Auto (Caldaire) and Shamrock & Rambler (Drawlane) respectively.

There were further moves into bus operation by National Express. Amberline of Liverpool, a contractor on National Express services, was purchased in mid-1989 and put under the control of Crosville Wales. It soon introduced local bus services in Liverpool.

The troubled ATL group disappeared in 1989. At

the start of the year its Crosville business was sold to Drawlane, then in mid-year the remainder was purchased by National Express. This gave National Express the SUT bus operations in Sheffield, plus the Carlton dealership with its Neoplan franchise. ATL's Leeds Airebus operations closed in the spring of 1989 before the National Express takeover.

After three months the SUT bus operation was sold by National Express to the mysterious Hallam Bus Co, allegedly owned by South Yorkshire Transport. SYT's

Above:
Wilts & Dorset has retained its independence and has one of the most distinctive liveries adopted by a former NBC fleet, using a bold combination of red, black and white. An ECW-bodied VRT, looking much smarter now than it did when delivered to West Yorkshire Road Car in NBC poppy red in 1979, arrives in Weymouth. It joined the Wilts & Dorset fleet in 1991.

Left:
The Badgerline group has been buying large numbers of Dennis Darts and Lances. A Dart with Plaxton bodywork is seen running in Swansea for South Wales Transport.

Right:
After a period of running a fleet made up almost entirely of minibuses, double-deckers started to reappear in the Milton Keynes City Bus fleet after its purchase by Cambus. This VRT, new to Eastern Counties, came from Viscount, the company formed in 1989 to run Cambus's Peterborough operation. Cambus ownership also brought a new red and cream livery to Milton Keynes to replace the insipid grey which was previously used.

denials of any involvement with the Hallam Bus Co sounded just a bit hollow when SYT took SUT over from Hallam in November.

Drawlane doubled in size in 1989. It gave up its south coast operations. Minibuses which were operated under the Charlie's Cars banner by Shamrock & Rambler had been abandoned at the end of 1988 after strong competition from Bournemouth Yellow Buses, while the S&R coach operation ceased in April with part of it being taken over by the new Dorset Travel Services company.

But Drawlane added Crosville, buying it from ATL in February and running it for 10 months before splitting it up. Part (including the former Yelloway bus operations) was added to Drawlane's Bee Line Buzz operation, purchased from Stagecoach in September. Crosville operations around Crewe were transferred to Midland Red North, while those in Warrington, Northwich and Runcorn went to North Western — both, of course, sister Drawlane subsidiaries. This left Crosville with around 150 buses. It had had 436 when acquired from ATL. The remaining Crosville fleet, serving Chester, Birkenhead and Ellesmere Port, was sold to PMT in February 1990. Ultimately Crosville buses acquired PMT's red and yellow livery. In exchange the PMT fleet adopted Crosville's anachronistic alpha-numeric fleet-numbering system.

Anachronistic, incidentally, is far from being a term of insult. Crosville's use of easily-understood vehicle type codes was an admirable scheme — but

few of its kind survived computerisation and the computer programmer's obsession with numbers at the expense of letters.

To its ownership of Midland Red North Drawlane added Midland Fox, previously Midland Red East. It also tried to establish a toehold in Sheffield, an area of intense competition, making overtures to the small SheafLine company in the autumn of 1989. SheafLine had been set up at the end of 1988 by former SYT employees but was running into difficulties. Drawlane got as far as loaning SheafLine 10 North Western Atlanteans (some of which were repainted in SheafLine colours), but SYT had more than enough trouble on the streets of Sheffield without one of the major groups coming in and so took over SheafLine itself.

Another abortive competitive foray saw Midland Red North launch minibus services in Derby in mid-1989, competing with Derby City Transport. This operation, with 34 vehicles, was sold to Derby City Transport in early 1990 — so in the end there might have been some pay-off from the sale of buses, if not from the carriage of passengers.

From around 1,000 buses at the start of the 1989, Drawlane's fleet had doubled to just over 2,000 at the end. There were other takeovers too in 1989. The most significant included Trent's acquisition of Barton Transport, Western Travel buying G&G of Leamington and Proudmutual buying Moor-Dale Coaches and R&M. All were examples of erstwhile NBC companies buying established independents.

An interesting tactical acquisition was that of the Tyne & Wear Omnibus Company — TWOC — by Go-Ahead Northern. TWOC had been set up in 1987 by Trimdon Motor Services to compete in Newcastle-upon-Tyne with Busways. TMS was unwilling to sell it to Busways, but reached a deal with Go-Ahead — who immediately resold it to Busways, no doubt to the chagrin of its original owners. Ironically, the term TWOC is widely used in the northeast in relation to car theft: taking without owner's consent. The same could be said of TWOC's acquisition by Busways.

1990: some winners, some losers

If the badger had been asleep in 1988 and 1989, it emerged from its slumbers in 1990. At the start of the year it was running 1,500 vehicles. By the end it had 2,500. This was achieved by the takeover of South Wales Transport and its associated companies in February, followed by Eastern National in April, and Wessex Coaches of Bristol in June. All were ex-NBC MBOs. Eastern National was quickly divided in two, with services in south Essex and London passing to a new Thamesway company in July.

AJS continued to cut back in 1990. Part of its Sovereign operation in Stevenage was sold to Luton & District, although in partial compensation there was expansion on LRT tendered services in Harrow. Control of most of County Bus & Coach passed to Lynton Travel, in effect a buyout by the company's chairman, Bob Howells — whose middle name is Lynton. County's Grays operations, trading as Thameside, were retained by AJS. Part of this was sold to Grey-Green early in 1991, with the remainder

Above:
The new-look Crosville in PMT red and yellow livery. An Optare Delta offloads in Chester bus station. It carries the Crosville name above the windows.

Stagecoach is easily the biggest, and the only one to have a corporate livery — which is as controversial now as NBC's was almost 25 years ago. Badgerline has gone for a more subtle approach, with its subsidiaries retaining their own liveries but with the addition of a smiling badger logo. British Bus has as yet done nothing to tell the world that it's a major group.

The successors to two one-time PTE operators — MTL and West Midlands Travel — are expanding although only WMT has acquired ex-NBC operations, to which it has added a WM prefix. Quite what that means to a bus passenger in Harlow boarding a WM County bus is anybody's guess. But one thing is certain. The operations around London have finally shaken off any vestiges of being London Transport's Country Area, an aura which clung to them even under NBC ownership.

The real question now is what happens to the new groups. Can small operations like Blazefield, Transit Holdings and Yorkshire Traction survive? Will even the biggest groups remain separate? That the big groups are themselves subject to change was graphically demonstrated in the summer of 1995 when Badgerline and GRT Bus Group merged to form First Bus.

Look back 10 years and who would have forecast that the biggest single slice of NBC would come to be owned by a Perthshire express coach operator? That Eastern Counties would be controlled from Aberdeen? Or that what was for a time the biggest bus company in Wales would vanish without trace?

Indeed, NBC itself is vanishing without trace. There are still a few depots and offices displaying signs with either the double-N logo or NBC-style lettering which nobody has bothered to take down. And for a few years to come there will be the legacy of NBC's vehicle buying policy. Gradually-dwindling numbers of apparently indestructible Leyland Nationals continue to serve all too many English towns and cities. Bristol VRTs and the Leyland Olympians which succeeded them look to be with us for some time yet.

The new groups are investing in new buses. Badgerline has been buying Dennis Darts and Lances. Stagecoach is majoring on Volvo B10Ms and Olympians. British Bus is taking Darts, as is the Go-Ahead Group. GRT Bus Group has ploughed an independent furrow, with Scanias and full-size Mercedes-Benz single-deckers.

The pace of change has been remarkable. No one can tell what the future holds. But it's a fair bet that by the year 2000 we'll have seen a few more surprises as the shake-up continues in Britain's buses.

Where are they now?

A list of the original purchasers of NBC's bus and coach operating subsidiaries, arranged in order of sale, with details of their current ownership.

Company	Original buyer	Present owner
Devon General	MBO	no change
Badgerline	MBO	First Bus
Southern Vectis	MBO	no change/PLC
Cheltenham & Gloucester	MBO	Stagecoach
Maidstone & District	MBO	British Bus
Cambus	MBO	no change
PMT	MBO	First Bus
South Midland	MBO	absorbed by Transit Holdings
Midland Red West	MBO	First Bus
Midland Red Coaches	Midland Red West	First Bus
Eastern National	MBO	First Bus
Trent	MBO	no change
City of Oxford	MBO	Go-Ahead Group
Yorkshire Traction	MBO	British Bus
West Riding/YWD	MBO	British Bus
National Travel East	ATL	Mainline
East Yorkshire	MBO	no change
Eastern Counties	MBO	First Bus
East Kent	MBO	Stagecoach
Hampshire Bus	Stagecoach	no change
Pilgrim Coaches	Stagecoach	closed
National Welsh	MBO	closed
Northern General	MBO	no change
Provincial	Employee buyout	no change
Brighton & Hove	MBO	Go-Ahead Group
South Wales Transport	MBO	First Bus
Wilts & Dorset	MBO	no change
Shamrock & Rambler	Drawlane	closed
Cumberland	Stagecoach	no change
Wessex National	MBO	First Bus
Western National	Plympton/Badgerline	First Bus
Milton Keynes City Bus	MBO	Cambus
Midland Fox	MBO/Stevensons	British Bus
Luton & District	MBO	British Bus
West Yorkshire	MBO	Yorkshire Rider/Blazefield
Bristol Omnibus	Midland Red West	First Bus
Voyage National	Eastern National	closed
Southdown	MBO	Stagecoach
Northumbria	MBO	British Bus
Alder Valley South	Frontsource	British Bus/Stagecoach
United Counties	Stagecoach	no change
United Auto	Caldaire	West Midlands Travel
Ambassador Travel	MBO	no change
Midland Red South	Western Travel	Stagecoach
Berks Bucks Bus Co	Q Drive	Q Drive/British Bus/Reading Transport
Hastings & District	MBO	Stagecoach
Crosville Wales	MBO	British Bus
London Country North West	MBO	British Bus/Q Drive
Midland Red North	Drawlane	no change
Lincolnshire	Yorkshire Traction	no change
East Midland	MBO	Stagecoach
London Country South West	Drawlane	no change
Ribble	MBO	Stagecoach
Kentish Bus	Proudmutual	British Bus
North Western	Drawlane	no change
Crosville	ATL	First Bus
Southern National	MBO	no change
North Devon	MBO	no change
London Country North East	AJS	West Midlands Travel

Wider horizons

Groups whose strength has been built on the purchase of former NBC subsidiaries have expanded by buying other companies. The most significant expansions in England are:

Stagecoach
Barrow Borough Transport operations
Busways Travel Services
Cleveland Transit
Darlington Transport operations
East London Bus & Coach Co
Grimsby-Cleethorpes Transport
Hartlepool Transport
Kingston-upon-Hull City Transport
Lancaster City Transport operations
Mainline group (20% share)
Selkent

British Bus
Colchester Borough Transport
Derby City Transport
Southend Transport

Badgerline
Yorkshire Rider

Go-Ahead group
London Central

Wider than the Y

There was a lot more to the Scottish Bus Group's vehicle policy than the ubiquitous Y-type. **Alan Millar** takes a look.

buses and coaches, putting it close behind London Transport in the big operator league table, but even if it had wanted to follow LT's rigid buying policies, its operating requirements wouldn't have allowed it. Scotland is a country of polarised populations. A densely populated central belt, sparsely populated Highlands and Southern Uplands. Most towns are small by English standards and support connecting rather than self-contained bus services.

Add a short summer season to that mix and you see why the most useful buses were dual purpose single-deckers offering comfort for longer interurban journeys and which could be used for the short summer peak coaching requirements. But there also are remote rural areas where those buses were too big

If you thought the Scottish Bus Group's vehicle buying began and ended with the Alexander Y-type and some dubious 1960s Leyland-designed Albions over which discreet and dark veils ought to be drawn, read on. This might change your mind.

SBG certainly wasn't another Tilling with captive in-house chassis and body manufacturers like Bristol and ECW. Nor another London Transport laying down precise specifications for a highly standardised fleet. Not even another BET group whose windscreen designs are still bought by bus managers who may well never have heard of British Electric Traction.

But SBG was a formidable buyer which, despite yielding to the occasional temptation of designing its own buses, for the most part just went out and bought what it felt were the best buses available at a price it was prepared to pay. Maybe that put SBG ahead of its time, for this is the same approach taken by the private sector groups of the 1990s.

At its peak in the early 1970s, SBG ran over 4,500

Above and right:
Leyland vs AEC: 1 — both Tigers and Regals were purchased by SBG companies in the late 1940s. Alexander was the biggest user of Tigers and this one has a 35-seat Alexander body. Regals were bought by Alexander, Western SMT and Scottish Omnibuses, with the last-named being the biggest Regal user. Burlingham bus bodywork is fitted to this Regal III.
Stewart J. Brown collection

or some densely populated urban areas where they were too small or unnecessarily luxurious.

Those were the basic requirements of a group which began life in Edinburgh in 1906 as the Scottish Motor Traction Company and soon was better known by its initials SMT. It became a group after the LNER and LMS railways bought a half stake in SMT in August 1929 and set about expanding it into an empire of four companies covering most of Scotland — SMT, Central SMT, Western SMT and Alexander's.

Nationalisation led to further expansion and the creation of a fifth subsidiary, Highland Omnibuses, in March 1952. The group also began to change its name. The original SMT company retained its trading name until 1964, when it became Eastern Scottish, but the legal name became Scottish Omnibuses in 1949 and the group began to be referred to as the Scottish Omnibuses group and became Scottish Omnibuses Group (Holdings) Ltd in 1961. But as no self-respecting Scot with the possible exception of Edinburgh lawyers responsible for quaint company titles ever caught an 'omnibus', it was being called the Scottish Bus Group before that became its official name in 1963.

Each company had its own preferences and

power. Disappointed by its first purchases, it designed and built around 90 of its own Lothian single-deckers between 1913 and 1924, but this was merely a passing phase. Rather than follow London General and Midland Red into larger volume chassis manufacturing, SMT was soon relying on three manufacturers — Leyland, AEC and Bedford — as its combined fleet expanded.

By a huge margin, Leyland was the biggest supplier and right through the 1930s almost every model it built went to SMT fleets: Tigers, Titans, Lions, Lionesses, Cheetahs, Cubs, even rarities like six-wheel Gnus and the only underfloor-engined Panda. AEC met some of the original SMT company's needs and Bedford built coaches, but other

prejudices. Alexander's — split from 1961 into separate Fife, Midland and Northern companies — and SMT seemed closest to the heart of SBG thinking. Both had a mix of urban and rural, bus and coach operations and chose vehicles which met those needs.

Western SMT, made up of substantial ex-BET and Tilling interests, had a similar mix of routes, but the strong characters of founder manager John Sword and his son William set its vehicle-buying apart for much of its history. Central SMT, running profitable urban routes in Lanarkshire and Dunbartonshire, had little need for coaches or even DP single-deckers and took a spartan approach to what it bought. Highland, run initially as a remote offshoot of SMT, was a pauper among princes which relied on its rich neighbours for cast-offs to supplement the small numbers of buses it could afford to buy new. It took what it could get.

Right from the start, SMT exercised its buying

manufacturers — including Scottish-owned Albion — barely got a look in.

Most single-deck bodies came from Alexander's coachbuilding department in Stirling which was so busy it seldom had room for outside customers' needs. Burlingham, supplying mainly coaches, and Leyland, building small batches of double-deckers, were the other main body suppliers.

When war broke out, coaches were rebodied as double-deckers and utility 'deckers joined the fleets. While Bedford met all of the group's utility single-deck requirements with 187 OWBs, Leyland and AEC were out of the bus market and unfamiliar new makes of 'deckers came in the shape of 253 Guy Arabs, 40 Daimlers and a solitary Bristol K5G for Central.

Guy and Daimler reaped a postwar harvest. Guy supplied 196 Arab IIIs (mostly single-deckers), more than half of them to Alexander's, but none with

Alexander bodies, while Daimler contributed 112 single and double-deckers. But Daimler's reluctance to fit Gardner engines — a rarely discovered pre-war pleasure in SMT fleets — deprived it of the favour which Guy enjoyed and some were sold without being used.

The fondness for Guys was such that when London Transport started selling its 435 utility Arabs in the early 1950s, SBG — as a fellow British Transport Commission organisation — exercised its right of first refusal and took 132. Alexander's kept 43 in service with their original bodies, Western had 52 rebodied and disguised 25 of them as Arab IVs with tin fronts and 1953 Ayrshire registrations, while SMT rebuilt 23 as 30ft single-deckers, mostly for Highland Omnibuses.

Not that old friends were deserted. Leyland and AEC came back into favour as soon as their postwar products were available, but in different proportions from before. SMT bought Regents and Regals to the total exclusion of Leylands; Alexander's and Western bought batches of AECs for the first time and Central took a single Regent III for evaluation.

Indeed, AEC supplied more Regals than Leyland supplied Tigers between 1946 and 1951 and it was only through its dominance of double-deck deliveries that Leyland retained its main supplier status.

These purchases reveal one of the great characteristics of SBG vehicle policy. Conservatism. Given a choice, it usually preferred the simpler option, so it progressed from O662 Regals with crash gearboxes to Regal IIIs with preselective boxes, but reverted to crash boxes for the final deliveries of Regal IIIs. Of the Tigers, all but 20 for Alexander's were PS1s rather than PS2s.

Double-deck buying was just as conservative, with 37 more Titan PD1s than PD2s bought between 1946 and 1954, partly because of the influx of ex-London Guys in 1952/53 when PD2s might otherwise have been bought, but also because ultra-conservative Central, having bought 100 of the earliest PD2s in 1948, reverted to the less powerful PD1 and carried on buying them as late as 1951. One may mock, but Central's profits kept the rest of SBG afloat, so primitive buses also made money.

Even though it ceased to be part of the group in 1947, Alexander's coachworks remained the main body supplier for the next 40 years. It built nearly two thirds of the

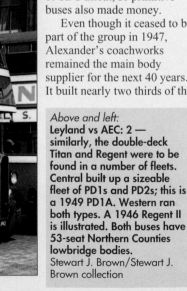

Above and left:
Leyland vs AEC: 2 — similarly, the double-deck Titan and Regent were to be found in a number of fleets. Central built up a sizeable fleet of PD1s and PD2s; this is a 1949 PD1A. Western ran both types. A 1946 Regent II is illustrated. Both buses have 53-seat Northern Counties lowbridge bodies.
Stewart J. Brown/Stewart J. Brown collection

half-cab single-deckers, rebodied many pre-war Tigers and Regals and, having entered the double-deck market in 1942, picked up a third of the 'decker orders, initially building Leyland designs before developing its own from 1951. Most SBG 'deckers had lowbridge bodies even where there were few low bridges.

Burlingham built most other single-deckers and Leyland became the second biggest double-deck body supplier, but Northern Counties capitalised on the success of its later utility Guys and bodied over 200 new 'deckers for Central and Western in the first eight postwar years, mainly on Regents and Titans.

Bedford supplied over 70 OB coaches, most with Duple Vista bodies assembled by the SMT Bedford dealership in Edinburgh, but Albion still was out of favour with its biggest potential native customer. Western bought 20 Venturers and Valiants and Alexander's got five Strachans-bodied Victors with petrol engines in 1950 — non-standard coaches which seem either to have been bought to meet an urgent requirement or became available through a BTC acquisition somewhere in Britain.

SBG overcame its innate conservatism and bought high capacity underfloor-engined single-deckers from 1951, initially on SMT and Western's prestigious overnight luxury coach services from Edinburgh and Glasgow to London. Picking up where it left off with the 1941 Leyland Panda, it bought 198 heavyweights by 1953 — 84 Leyland Royal Tigers, 58 AEC Regal IVs and 56 Guy Arab UFs. Central's Guys included SBG's last rear-entrance single-deckers.

They were followed over the next nine years by 1,005 lighter chassis, including almost twice as many AEC Reliances and Monocoaches as Leyland's less lively Tiger Cub. There also were small batches of 30ft Leopards, Albion Aberdonians — Glasgow-built ultra-lightweight Tiger Cubs — and Albion Nimbus coaches bought following trials with an integral midibus SMT built around Albion truck parts in 1955 — the last bus actually built by SBG. Western, impressed above all by Gardner engines, preserved the group's relationship with Guy until 1959 by taking the lion's share of 69 Arab LUFs.

Over 80% of these vehicles were bodied by Alexander to a succession of standard bus and coach designs culminating in 1962 with a modified version of its BET group body. There even were 100 Alexander-bodied Monocoaches, but the ACV group's ability to sell complete vehicles resulted in 113 Park Royal-bodied Reliances and Monocoaches being bought between 1954 and 1959. The only postwar Leyland coach bodies were on 10 1952 Royal Tigers for Alexander's.

Burlingham was virtually abandoned. Not a single underfloor-engined Seagull in the 1950s, just 42 new Bedford SBs for SMT and Alexander's, and new bodies on 20 SMT Bedford OBs and two Highland OWBs converted to forward control, and 48 SMT Regal Is and IIIs. Only in 1961, when Duple was taking over, did it body 11 Reliance coaches for SMT.

You can blame part of its fate on nationalisation. BTC ownership gave SBG access to Bristol and ECW products no longer available on the open market, so even though the group's experience of them only amounted to Central's sole Northern Counties-bodied K5G and 18 ECW-bodied Ls and Ks Western inherited in 1949 with Tilling's Scottish company, Caledonian, it was under pressure to buy.

As early as 1951, ECW

bodied Alexander's last 13 Daimler CVD6 coaches and over the next two years rebodied 40 double-deckers — 18 utility Guys for Western and Alexander's, three utility Daimlers, four prewar Albions and 15 five-year-old PD1s for Western. The original Strachans bodies on the PD1s had gone into self-destruct mode almost on their first day in service. Western also had 12 prewar Regals rebodied with ECW-style Brislington Bus Works double-deck bodies.

Bristol had to wait until 1954, when it supplied the first of 50 ECW-bodied LS6G and 20 MW6G coaches for SMT's touring fleet. Alexander's Fife fleet took 20 LS6G buses in 1955 to run alongside Guys, while Western achieved something no other nationalised fleet managed — 71 Alexander-bodied LSs and MWs delivered between 1957 and 1962.

But Bristol's real breakthrough came with the

LD Lodekka which not only ousted the Guy Arab as its choice of Gardner-engined 'decker, but was bought in bigger quantities than any other double-decker available at the time. When SBG switched to the flat-floor F-series in 1961, FLs were a particular rarity (two for Western) and Central took the only 48 FSFs in Scotland. For some inexplicable reason maybe tied up with available parts, most of the 101 FSs were

Top:
The nearest thing to a standard SBG double-decker in the 1960s was the attractive Alexander-bodied Fleetline. This one was operated by Alexander (Fife).
Stewart J. Brown

Middle:
A minority of SBG Fleetlines had ECW bodywork. These included 35 delivered to Central in 1971 which were quickly displaced to other SBG fleets.
Stewart J. Brown

Bottom:
The trusty Leyland Leopard was the workhorse of most SBG fleets. Over 1,500 were fitted with Alexander Y-type bodies and could be found the length and breadth of the country. This one was new in 1977 and was operated by Central.
Stewart J. Brown

bought in 1964 after the group had been taking FLFs for two years. They were the last rear-entrance buses built for SBG and 35 went to ultra conservative Central.

FLFs — like most SBG Bristols fitted with six cylinder Gardner engines — were bought until 1967, a year before production ended. All 376 had constant mesh gearboxes, but the last 126 for Central, Fife and Eastern Scottish were extra long 31ft versions, 83 of them for Central. This was almost an exclusively Scottish Lodekka, otherwise bought only by Eastern National which took 53 after the last SBG vehicles were built, but unlike Eastern National, SBG took full advantage of the extra length by squeezing in 76 or 78 seats.

Not that SBG stopped buying lowbridge 'deckers with sunken gangways.

While LDs were being bought, almost as many 59-seat PD2s and 67-seat PD3s with vacuum brakes and synchromesh gearboxes went to Central, Western and Alexander's and although many Lodekkas replaced highbridge buses, lowbridge Leylands were used on some busy routes around Glasgow.

Leyland wanted to convert SBG to the rear-engined wonders of the Atlantean, but not even big discounts would persuade it to buy. Leyland's chances were hardly advanced when Central, of all companies, briefly became Scotland's biggest Atlantean operator in 1961 when it acquired two with the Chieftain business of Laurie's of Hamilton. They stayed

Top:
Bedfords were bought for rural services by Scottish Omnibuses, but often ended up on other inappropriate duties as demonstrated by a Willowbrook-bodied VAM on the Glashow-Edinburgh express.
Stewart J. Brown

Left:
New high standards of comfort were brought to SBG's London services with the introduction of the double-glazed Alexander M-type, a coach ahead of its time. An Eastern Scottish Bristol REMH loads in Victoria Coach Station.
Stewart J. Brown

about seven years which turned out to be longer than SBG's preferred new Leyland lowheight 'decker lasted at Central.

This was the Lowlander, the first big partnership with Albion following Leyland's takeover in 1951. It was a cheaply developed forward-entrance lowheight PD3 which also was SBG's first bus with a semi-automatic gearbox — an option deleted on later deliveries — and Western, Central and the Alexander's fleets bought 194 between 1961 and early 1965.

To say they were a disaster would be an overstatement. More a disappointment. But Central loathed them so much that its 30 were repatriated within three years; 32 of Western's 111 were moved on just as quickly, in both cases to Fife (which had bought seven new and was able to absorb another 32) and Highland which presumably had little choice and, in any case, wasn't used to getting such new 'deckers. The Lowlander brought the group's association with 'real' Leyland 'deckers to an abrupt and ignominious end.

It also marked the end of Northern Counties' best years of SBG business. It bodied nearly 40% of the later PD2s and PD3s and more than a quarter of the Lowlanders, but by 1965 only Western was ordering its products. Park Royal met an urgent SMT order for 20 PD2s in 1957 and 23 Northern Counties-style PD3s for Western in 1960 were Burlingham's last bus bodies for SBG.

Eastern Scottish never ran Lowlanders, but was to enjoy — if that is the word — its own association with two of its rivals. Thanks to the takeover of Baxter's of Airdrie in 1962, it inherited a one-year-old AEC Bridgemaster and two brand new ones about to leave Park Royal's works. It got one of them; the other was sold to Red Rover of Aylesbury and was replaced by a Renown delivered during 1963 for evaluation with at least half an idea of buying more. It didn't catch on, all three lowheight AECs were shipped off to hapless Highland in the early 1970s and everyone assumed (wrongly) that SBG had bought its last AEC double-deckers.

The Baxter takeover did change SBG thinking. A Daimler Fleetline — the first with lowheight Alexander body — was on order and went on to the Edinburgh-Glasgow route along with the Renown and the customary Lodekkas. It moved on to Baxter routes, was burnt out, replaced by another identical bus and then the original was rebuilt. While Eastern Scottish showed no sign of buying any more, Western bought 55 Fleetlines in 1965 and restored the reputation of a manufacturer which had enjoyed fleeting postwar favour.

They were the first of 640 Fleetlines bought over the next 15 years. Even before one-person operation was being considered seriously, the benefits of higher capacity Gardner-engined 'deckers outweighed any worries about rear engines and Western, Midland and

Fife were all convinced of its virtues. Western even took seven 33ft 83-seaters in 1967 and might well have bought many more had Whitehall mandarins not omitted 33ft lowheights from the new bus grant scheme in 1968.

By the time SBG started buying Fleetlines, the single-deck body with which the group is most associated — the Alexander Y-type — was already becoming well established in its fleets. A sensation when it was launched in 1961, perhaps a tad dated when production ended in 1983, it fitted SBG's needs like a glove. Over 2,800 were bought new over those 22 years for every group fleet.

There were 10 and 11m versions, 38-seat London coaches in the early years, also some touring coaches, but mainly service buses and DPs. Most buses had short windows, most DPs had long windows with sloping pillars which captured the mood of the swinging sixties, but there also were DPs with little windows and buses with big ones. Highland got a mailbus with 24 seats and a huge freight compartment in the back. SBG bought them for so long that Y-types replaced Y-types.

Early deliveries included Midland's last Tiger Cubs; the group's last Reliances in 1966; all 228 rear-engined Albion Vikings bought between 1965 and 1970, mainly for the three Alexander companies' rural routes; 66 Bristol RELHs (mainly London coaches) for Eastern and Western in 1966 and 27 front-engined Bedford VAMs for Highland and Eastern Scottish. But the chassis most associated with the Y-type was the 11m Leyland Leopard, of which 1,550 were built from 1963. Almost a third of them went to Western, nearly as many to Central which only took 53-seat short window buses — in the early days to replace 53-seat lowbridge PD1s and PD2s.

Bedford was still meeting the group's need for small buses and coaches, supplying 65 VASs — 45 Duple-bodied coaches (mainly for Highlands and Islands tours restricted by narrow roads, weak bridges and compact ferries) and 20 with Willowbrook (Duple Group) bus bodies — as well as bigger Duple-bodied SBs and VAMs for Central, Midland and Northern. Highland and Eastern bought 25 Willowbrook-bodied VAMs in 1968.

At the other end of the spectrum, SBG was setting new standards in 1968 on its overnight London services. Keen to take advantage of the new 12m length limit, it tested Mercedes-Benz and Magirus Deutz coaches, went abroad to see coaches like the legendary American Greyhounds and ended up designing a British Greyhound lookalike whose specification still looks good a quarter century later.

This was the Alexander M-type, a 42-seater based initially on 70 Bristol REMH chassis bought in 1968-71 and fitted with double-glazed trapezoid windows, reclining seats, a toilet (a standard SBG London feature since 1951), night heaters, air suspension and stacks of luggage space. Maybe

Alexander compromised too much by fitting bus windscreens, but the M-type was an impressive and effective tool of its trade. A further 26, on steel-sprung mid-engined chassis, were bought in 1975/76.

The first M-types came as SBG went through a crucial change. Controlled from London for 20 years — first by BTC, then by the Transport Holding Company which also ran the Tilling companies and held the state's stake in Bristol and ECW — it was transferred to the Edinburgh-based Scottish Transport Group in January 1969 and THC's interest in Bristol and ECW passed to the National Bus Company. SBG was no longer under the same obligation to buy from either manufacturer.

It also got its first group engineering director. Roddy MacKenzie, after over 30 years in the industry, 13 as Eastern Scottish general manager, changed the course of SBG's bus buying. Like an Islamic fundamentalist denouncing decadence from his minaret, MacKenzie railed against rear engines, semi-automatic gearboxes, low floors and power steering and his appointment ushered in a period of basic buses with mid and front engines, manual gearboxes, high floors and steering gear that demanded drivers with Arnold Schwarzenegger's arms. And its last Bristols.

Twelve ECW-bodied RELL6Gs bought by Fife in 1968 remained the group's only low frame single-deckers for nine years, but their fate may have more to do with the last double-deckers delivered to Eastern Scottish before MacKenzie's promotion. Central had been testing one of the in-line-engined VRX prototypes, but when the transverse-engined VRT was developed hurriedly to meet industry demands, Eastern got the first 25 — 33ft 83-seaters ordered before the bus grant rules were announced. Before they were delivered, SBG ordered another 84 standard length VRTs for Eastern, Central, Western and Midland.

If 25 inadequately developed new buses in a fleet with only two rear-engined 'deckers was asking for trouble, putting them into one run by someone who loathed their every feature amounted to a kiss of death. Obligingly, those first VRTs lived up to MacKenzie's worst fears. They were dogged by cooling and transmission problems and substantial pre-delivery rectification work had to be carried out on the next 84.

The group turned to a new combination of ECW-bodied Fleetlines from 1970, but in rapidly diminishing quantities, and although Bristol announced its improved Series 2 VRT that year, SBG didn't want to know. By 1974, 106 of the VRTs had been swapped for late-model crash gearbox FLFs in NBC fleets and Western had found buyers for the other three. The

a long lasting all-round bus which would see several group companies through the difficult privatisation years. Although SBG's 1985 restructure into 11 regional companies scattered them more widely, the 518 Pennine VIIs were only delivered to Western and Eastern Scottish.

Following MacKenzie's retirement, group policy began to be relaxed and Leopards and Pennine VIIs came with semi and fully-automatic gearboxes and power steering.

Alexander launched its T-type body in 1974 to try and restore some of the Y-type's lost coaching appeal, but although 242 were bought (mainly Seddons), many group companies required proper coaches, mostly about 200 Duple Dominants, but also 64 Plaxton Supremes on Eastern Scottish Seddons — the first Scarborough products the group ordered. It turned to Plaxton in 1978 when Alexander's coachworks were stretched to capacity.

When Eastern Scottish ran so short of serviceable buses in 1977 that it bought a dozen 15-year-old PD2s from Lothian, Tom Marsden, the former Grampian transport director who had succeeded MacKenzie's successor, seized the opportunity to introduce his new colleagues to the virtues of the Leyland National which could be delivered at short notice. Ten went on to former Baxter routes before the end of 1977 and by 1981, 68 Mark 1 and 136 Leyland-engined Mark 2 Nationals were bought by every company except Western which was unimpressed by the lack of a Gardner option.

The National fell from favour as SBG stepped up its double-deck purchases, partly to make up for buying so few in the MacKenzie years and later as market analysis reviews threw up a need for more high-capacity buses. Back in 1973, Ailsa Bus had developed its revolutionary front-engined 'decker very much with SBG in mind and Midland had tried the highbridge Volvo-engined prototype early the following year. Had it heeded MacKenzie's advice, Ailsa would have built an updated FLF Lodekka so it had to earn SBG's business, but was rewarded by a 1975 order for 40 from Fife which had run highbridge Guys five years earlier.

Highland and Northern were all set to get 18 lowheight Ailsas in 1976. Alas, the prototype for

relationship with Bristol finally ended in 1972, following the delivery of 75 none-too-highly-regarded Perkins-engined LHs — the only LHs bodied by Alexander — to Midland and Eastern Scottish.

With Bristol out of favour and AEC and Daimler absorbed into British Leyland, SBG needed new suppliers, but its options were limited. Alexander-bodied Ford R-Series (66 Willowbrook-bodied R192s had been bought off-the-peg by Highland from the mid-1960s) and Bedford Y-Series — cheap, light, basic chassis from manufacturers independent of BL — met MacKenzie's criteria and were bought initially as rural buses, later less successfully for anything from express to town services.

For heavier duty work, MacKenzie commissioned the Seddon Pennine VII — arguably the most successful bus ever designed for SBG. Seddon used proprietary components to create the nearest equivalent to a Leopard with a Gardner 6HLXB engine which, despite the limitations of its high floor, turned out to be

Derby was such a dog's breakfast that more Fords were bought instead, but the group began to realise highbridge buses could be used more widely. By 1980, five fleets ran 154 Ailsas with Alexander AV bodies.

The Fleetline was back in favour, too. By 1980, 168 Leyland-badged models had been delivered, including 23 for Northern and Highland which were enjoying spin-offs from the North Sea oil boom. ECW bodied nearly half of them, but Western bought 50 from Northern Counties in 1978, its last buses for SBG.

Under Marsden's influence, Fife ordered three Leyland Titans, Midland three Alexander-bodied lowheight MCW Metrobuses and Central an Alexander-bodied Dennis Dominator. The Metrobuses were the group's first MCW products and the Dominator was its first Dennis since 1942. But the Titans were axed along with the Park Royal factory and Midland got a prototype ECW-bodied Olympian in 1980.

No single new generation 'decker took the group's fancy, so it bought the lot. More than half of its last 510 new 'deckers were Olympians and Metrobuses, but it also took Dominators, Mk3 Ailsas and underfloor-engined Volvo Citybuses and

Leyland/DAB Lions. Most had Alexander R-type bodies, but ECW bodied 41 Eastern and Northern Olympians in 1982, ending a 31-year association with SBG.

In total contrast with its past, the group bought fewer full-size single-deckers than double-deckers in its last 10 years. But the vast majority were Leylands, 315 Tigers bought eagerly as soon as it was launched in 1981 to replace the less powerful Leopard. Most had Leyland engines, but Western, Central and Northern took sizeable numbers with Gardner engines, an option Leyland developed to carry on SBG's Seddon tradition and as a reaction to Dennis's success in selling 44 Dorchesters to Western and Central. Western's independence limited its Tiger intake to just 26, while it alone bought 35 Volvo B10Ms to join eight M-type B58s put on London services in 1975. It even took four with Dutch-built Berkhof bodies, the only imported coach bodies the group bought new.

Alexander bodied nearly half of these vehicles, mostly with the restyled T-type family introduced in 1982, but Northern and Fife opted for the Y-type's slab-sided P-type successor. Central, still locked in PD1 thinking, tried to forget it had ever bought Nationals by taking steel sprung, heavily derated Tigers and had 68 of these and five Dorchesters fitted with the only TS-type bus bodies Alexander built — complete with higher floors than its 400 Y-type Leopards.

Duple built most of the coaches. It outbid Alexander to build M-type replacements and was persuaded to incorporate trapezoid windows into the Dominant III and high-floor Goldliner III which, unlike the M-type, were sold to many other operators. SBG graduated on to standard Laser, Caribbean, 320 and 340 bodies and also continued its newer association with Plaxton by taking Paramounts on a range of chassis.

The group seemed prepared to try just about any new British coach on the market. There were 20 MCW Metroliners (11 of them double-deckers), eight Leyland Royal Tiger Doyens and three Duple 425 integrals. Western also bought three Plaxton-bodied Scania K112 double-deckers.

Northern embarked on a fruitless quest to find a rural bus successor to the Ford R-Series. The very last Y-types built in 1982 were a front-engined Volvo B57 (one of only two imported to the UK) and a Dennis Lancet with mid-mounted Perkins

Top left:
Leyland's initial reluctance to fit Gardner engines to its Tiger chassis opened the door for Dennis to supply its Dorchester to both Central and Western. This is a Plaxton-bodied coach in the Western fleet. *Stewart J. Brown*

Below left:
Ex-London Routemasters were used as part of their deregulation strategy by Clydeside, Kelvin and Strathtay — three of the four new companies created in the run-up to deregulation in 1986. Clydeside and Kelvin were the most enthusiastic Routemaster users. *Stewart J. Brown*

Above:
The Leyland Tiger succeeded the Leopard as the standard SBG coach. It came with a choice of power — Leyland, Gardner or Cummins. This Eastern Scottish example had a Leyland TL11 engine and a Duple 340 body. *Stewart J. Brown*

Left:
MCW Metrobuses were bought by Alexander (Midland), but with Alexander bodywork in place of the standard MCW-built body. This unusual combination is seen in Kilsyth.
Stewart J. Brown

V8 engine. The Volvo was the group's longest and lowest Y-type, the Dennis about its highest. Five more Lancets with P-type bodies followed, but all six were among the first Northern buses sold after Stagecoach bought the company in 1991. Need one say more?

Having collected 80 of SBG's Nationals into its fleet, the new Kelvin company bought an early Leyland Lynx in 1986 for evaluation. It remained a one-off as Kelvin's deregulation strategy went wrong and the group sold off some newer buses including Nationals and Metrobuses.

Deregulation also introduced nearly 300 midibuses in the group's last years. Most of its rural midis had gone by then, with Eastern Scottish and the new Lowland company using Reeve Burgess-bodied VASs and a 1989 Leyland Swift (the last decent-sized new bus the group bought) for special services in the Borders, while Central had met limited midibus requirements with VAS coaches, Alexander S-type integrals and finally a pair of Duple-bodied Leyland Cubs.

Apart from a couple of Sherpas for a rural route and three six-wheel Talbots for a dial-a-ride contract, it missed out on the bread van class of minibuses and took 212 Renault S56s mainly with Alexander bodies, 43 Alexander-converted Mercedes-Benz 608Ds and 24 MCW Metroriders.

But there was one other important final phase of SBG bus buying. A return to second-hand double-deckers on a scale unseen since nationalisation. It started in 1981 as new bus grant was being phased out and cheap modern buses became available and grew with the demands of deregulation. There were 61 London Transport, Tayside, Grampian, West Midlands and Greater Manchester Fleetlines; 25 South Yorkshire Ailsas and 15 Grampian Atlanteans — the group's first AN68s.

This was but a prelude to one of the most surprising episodes in SBG's 85-year history, its purchase of 166 AEC Routemasters from London Buses. This wasn't another retreat to old-fashioned buses, but the newly-created Clydeside, Kelvin and Strathtay companies' belief that fast open-platform 'deckers would win passengers in Glasgow and Dundee. Clydeside borrowed RM652 for an open day in 1985, kept it and built up a fleet of 76. Kelvin got 68, Strathtay 22 and others were bought to break for parts. They didn't deliver the commercial results SBG expected, but that was down to the strength of the group's competitors, not to the Routemasters themselves.

Their ranks were being thinned as SBG began to be privatised in 1990 but in May 1991, a few months before its sale consigned the group to the history books, Western bought SBG's last-ever buses for additional routes in Dumfries. Not new, nor typical of anything the company had run before, these were eight ex-Greater Manchester Atlanteans. But given that SMT's first buses had been double-deckers, there was a neat symmetry in these events.

SBG's successors — mainly Stagecoach, GRT, SB Holdings and Yorkshire Traction in 1994 — will work with their inheritence of group-purchased vehicles for many years to come and you could argue that Stagecoach's Alexander and Plaxton-bodied Volvos and Dennises — especially the conservative choice of B10M PSs rather than B10B Striders — continue the SBG tradition. From his celestial cloud, Roddy MacKenzie may allow himself the wry satisfaction that his legacy survives him.

Main single-deck purchases 1946-51

	AEC Regal	Leyland Tiger	Guy Arab	Daimler CVD 6	Body Totals
Alexander	142	250	—	—	392
Burlingham	120	63	—	51	234
Guy	—	—	84	—	84
Duple	50	—	30	—	80
Brockhouse	—	—	21	—	21
Massey	—	—	20	—	20
ECW	—	—	—	13	13
Brush	10	—	—	—	10
Chassis totals	**322**	**313**	**155**	**64**	**854**

Main double-deck purchases 1946-51

	Leyland PD1	Leyland PD2	AEC Regent	Daimler CVA/CVG	Guy Arab	Albion Venturer	Body totals
Alexander	82	78	60	24	—	18	262
Leyland	93	137	—	—	—	—	230
N Counties	77	10	89	24	7	—	207
Craven	—	—	—	—	25	—	25
Burlingham			20				20
Duple	—	—	20	—	—	—	20
Guy	—	—	—	—	16	—	16
Strachan	15	—	—	—	—	—	15
Chassis totals	267	225	189	48	48	18	795

Main single-deck purchases 1951-70

	Leyland Royal Tiger	Leyland Tiger Cub	Leyland Leopard	AEC Regal IV	AEC Reliance/ Monocoach	Guy	Bristol LS/MW RE	Albion	Ford	Bedford VAM/SB	Body totals
Alexander	74	249	26	58	409	125	71	47	—	—	1,059
Alexander Y	—	31	306	—	237	—	66	228	—	27	895
Alexander M	—	—	—	—	—	—	24	—	—	—	24
Park Royal	—	—	—	—	113	—	—	—	—	—	113
ECW	—	—	—	—	—	—	102	—	—	—	102
Duple	—	—	—	—	—	—	—	—	—	46	46
Willowbrook	—	—	—	—	—	—	—	—	17	25	42
Burlingham	—	—	—	—	11	—	—	—	—	—	11
Leyland	10	—	—	—	—	—	—	—	—	—	10
Chassis totals	84	280	332	58	770	125	263	275	17	98	2,302

Main double-deck purchases 1955-70

	Leyland PD2/PD3	Albion Lowlander	Guy Arab	Bristol Lodekka	AEC	Daimler Fleetline	Bristol VRT	Body totals
ECW	—	—	—	1,105	—	—	109	1,214
Alexander	302	142	13	—	—	259	—	716
N Counties	227	52	26	—	—	16	—	321
Burlingham	23	—	—	—	—	—	—	23
Park Royal	20	—	—	—	2	—	—	22
Chassis totals	572	194	39	1,105	2	275	109	2,296

Main single-deck purchases 1970-88

	Leyland Leopard	Leyland Tiger	Leyland National	Seddon	Bristol RE/LH	Ford	Bedford Y-series	Dennis	Volvo	Body totals
Alexander Y	1,244	—	—	288	75	232	121	1	1	1,962
Alexander M	12	—	—	6	46	—	—	—	8	72
Alexander T	65	17	—	160	—	—	—	—	—	242
Alexander TE	—	34	—	—	—	—	—	5	—	39
Alexander TS	—	68	—	—	—	—	—	5	—	73
Alexander TC	—	21	—	—	—	—	—	11	—	32
Alexander P	—	28	—	—	—	—	—	5	—	33
Leyland	—	—	204	—	—	—	—	—	—	204
Duple	90	108	—	—	—	118	11	—	22	349
Willowbrook	—	—	—	—	—	49	—	—	—	49
Plaxton	—	39	—	64	—	—	—	23	9	135
Berkhof	—	—	—	—	—	—	—	—	4	4
Chassis totals	1,411	315	204	518	121	399	132	50	44	3,194

Main double-deck purchases 1970-88

	Fleetline	Olympian	Ailsa	Metrobus	Dominator	Citybus	Lion	Body totals
Alexander	97	157	192	139	75	45	19	724
ECW	204	42	—	—	—	—	—	246
N Counties	64	—	—	—	—	—	—	64
Chassis totals	365	199	192	139	75	45	19	1,034

IT PAYS TO ADVERTISE —
SOMETIMES

Gavin Booth looks back at some of the advertising that was used to promote buses and coaches in the 1960s.

Picture the scene. It is 1964 and the bus company general manager is sitting at his mahogany desk, square-jawed, pipe in hand, poring over the latest copy of *Bus & Coach*. His eye alights on an advertisement for the Daimler Roadliner. He admires the tasteful artwork and reads the convincing copy. He sits upright and mutters 'By Jove, we must buy some of these.' He jabs a button on the large wooden box to his right and barks 'Get me Coventry 27626!'

It doesn't really ring true, does it? Surely nobody believes that bus operators make their buying decisions on the strength of an impressive advertisement in the trade press. But if that's the case, why do bus manufacturers advertise?

Is it because they have a new model to promote? Maybe. Is it to keep their name in front of potential customers? Perhaps. Is it because their advertising agencies convinced them to? Probably. Is it because everybody else does? Almost certainly.

Advertising for new buses and coaches peaked at the time of the postwar travel boom, around 1950, when there were more chassis and body manufacturers touting their wares than at any time since. As the market settled down and the bus industry set off on the long road of passenger decline, so many of the more marginal players dropped by the wayside and left it to the big boys. But as the industry moved through the acquisitive 1960s and even the big boys started to

disappear, then there was really only one advertiser of note: Leyland.

And this did nothing for the fortunes of the trade press, leading to the demise of *Bus & Coach* and doubtless contributing to the disappearance of others.

Bus & Coach was probably the best of the trade monthlies, and old copies are as useful today for the many pages of adverts as they are for the editorial content. A look back through the copies covering the 1960s is most revealing, and a fascinating reminder of the great changes that affected the bus manufacturing industry during that decade — longer vehicles; rear-engined single-deckers; the apparently unstoppable expansion of British Leyland.

Trade magazines rely on advertising to survive. *Bus & Coach* consistently had more pages of advertising that editorial. Sometimes considerably more. Its October/November 1950 issue, a bumper issue to coincide with the second postwar Commercial

RELIANCE
ABOVE ALL!...

Everybody looks up to the A.E.C. "Reliance". Operators, who choose it for outstanding comfort, reliability and operating economy. Coach rally judges, who year after year pick out the "Reliance" for premier awards. Body-builders everywhere, who have used the alternative 18' 7" wheelbase to give even greater luxury or increased passenger revenue. Available—as shown here—with air suspension and with alternative engines—the '470' giving 138 b.h.p. at 2,200 r.p.m. and the '590' 153 b.h.p. Designed and manufactured by A.E.C.

A.E.C. LIMITED
SOUTHALL · MIDDLESEX

Motor Show, had 140 pages of adverts to 48 pages of
editorial, but by the time the 1962 show came around
the adverts had dropped to 80 pages, and by the 1968
show it was down to 46 pages. The February 1970
issue had only 10 pages of advertising and was the
last-ever edition of *Bus & Coach* as a separate
magazine. After that it was merged into its truck-
dominated sister *Motor Transport*.

So what was around to be advertised in 1960? The
main single-deck competitors were the AEC Reliance
and Leyland Tiger Cub, with models from Atkinson,
Daimler, Dennis, Guy and Seddon on the lists but
selling in small numbers. Leyland's Leopard had just
appeared on the scene. The Bedford SB dominated the
lightweight coach market, with the Commer Avenger
on its way out and the Thames Trader on its way in.
This was the decade when buses grew from 30ft to
39ft 4in long, so small single-deckers were very rare.
There was the Albion Nimbus, and the Bedford VAS
would soon appear but there was very little else.

The double-decker was still almost universally
front-engined — AEC Regent V and Bridgemaster,
Daimler CV series, Dennis Loline III, Guy Arab IV
and Wulfrunian, Leyland Titan — but Leyland's rear-
engined Atlantean was beginning to pick up orders,
and Daimler was waiting in the wings with the
Fleetline.

Bristol was still state-owned and could build only
for other state-owned companies, so there was no need
to advertise.

Of the major manufacturers AEC, Daimler and
Leyland were the most prolific advertisers, which
reflected their importance in the market, but they each
chose very different ways to push their products.

AEC seemed to have no clear direction. For a time
it appeared to be just as likely to promote its export
successes ('In Lisbon they put their trust in fine British
automobile engineering') as it was to promote the
models that most *Bus & Coach* readers might actually
buy. So in between adverts for the new 36ft long
Reliance in 1961, the Renown in 1962, the Swift in
1964 and the Sabre in 1968, there were constant
reminders of the company's export successes (in the
days when British manufacturers regularly had export
successes) and some slightly more quirky ads that

Opposite:
**A simple, effective AEC advert for the Reliance, featuring
a Yelloway example with Harrington Cavalier bodywork.
ALL EXAMPLES FROM THE AUTHOR'S COLLECTION**

Top:
**Daimler made great play of its success in winning the first
'outside' order for Midland Red double-deckers to be
placed for some years. Previous Midland Red double-
deckers had been built by the operator itself.**

Left:
**Simms adapted what was very obviously a Sheffield AEC
Regent V/Park Royal to represent an anonymous double-
decker in this 1964 advert.**

Improving the service

London Transport's new plans envisage a much greater use of one-man-operated services. It means that more buses, like this country area Pay As You Enter vehicle, will soon be working on suburban red bus routes. For more than 50 years London Transport has been built upon AEC buses. To date nearly 23,000 vehicles have been supplied.

designed, engineered and manufactured by AEC LIMITED SOUTHALL MIDDLESEX

versatile ATLANTEAN!

LEYLAND'S 78-SEATER WITH PEAK PERFORMANCE

The Leyland Atlantean is versatile. Throughout Britain, the capacious Atlantean double-decker has proved itself able to meet peak period requirements and to operate economically on a variety of urban schedules. The Atlantean is fast becoming the most popular double-decker for municipal services.

The Atlantean's specification includes the famous Leyland O.680 diesel, rear mounted and easily accessible; optional dropped rear axle chassis permitting low overall height; automatic or semi-automatic gearbox, as required. This design makes possible a variety of one-stop, easy-entry and quick-exit bodies with alternative seating plans.

LEYLAND MOTORS LIMITED
Head Office & Home Sales: Leyland, Lancs. Tel: Leyland 21400 & 21661
OVERSEAS SALES: BERKELEY SQUARE HOUSE, BERKELEY SQUARE, LONDON, W.1. Tel GROsvenor 6050

suggested a change of agency or at least a change of copywriter.

The August 1964 *Bus & Coach* front cover features copy built around London Transport's orders for experimental buses: 'London Transport's new plans envisage a much greater use of one-man-operated services. It means that more buses, like this country area Pay As You Enter vehicle, will soon be working on suburban routes.' The colour photo illustrating the ad shows a 12-year old RF and as we know, the new buses for London were nothing like RFs. Perhaps if they had been...

The reason for AEC's odd choice of an older model to publicise the London orders becomes clear in the next issue, when two colour pages are devoted to the 'Brilliant New Bus/Coach Chassis', the Swift, described as 'The greatest step forward in underfloor engine bus/coach design' and as 'a triumph of engineering design'. AEC pushed the Swift hard right through the 1960s, the last ad appearing in July 1969 when Leyland was preparing the way for the launch of the National the following year and had probably got the message that the Swift didn't quite live up to the copywriter's glowing prose.

The copywriters really went for broke in 1965 with a couple of ads that were almost all copy, with little illustration. One purports to be a report of a 70mph 'duel' between a sports car and an AEC Reliance coach on the M1 motorway: 'We were checking speedometer calibrations at the time against those scientifically spaced motorway mile-posts. That didn't help soften the shock when a sudden horn-blast and a blaze of light behind announced that one of AEC's mighty Reliance diesel express coaches was pulling out to pass.' The writer's sports car has 150bhp on tap, but 'the giant air-sprung inter-city express up ahead boasted just three more horsepower from a massive, easy-

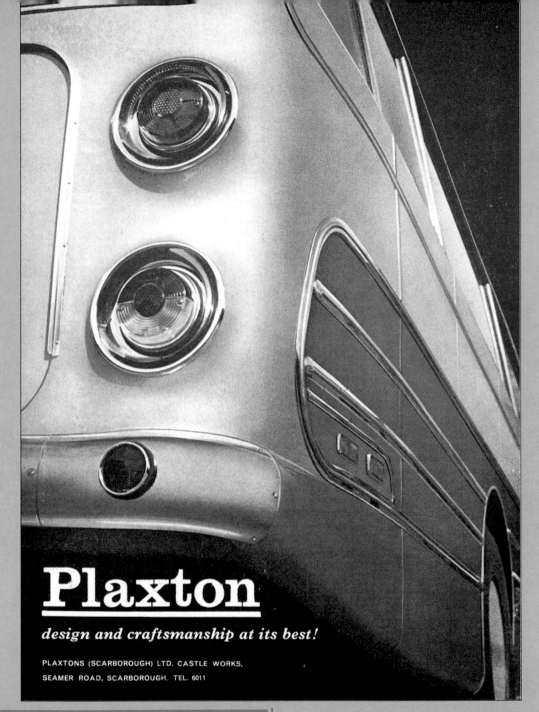

Plaxton

design and craftsmanship at its best!

PLAXTONS (SCARBOROUGH) LTD. CASTLE WORKS,
SEAMER ROAD, SCARBOROUGH. TEL. 6011

revving lightly stressed horizontal diesel six designed to go 100,000 hard highway miles between overhauls.' The 'lithe green two-seater' got past the Reliance in the end, 'exchanging gay thumbs-ups with the driver as we shifted briskly into top and accelerated away.' In spite of ads like this, the Reliance continued to be a steady seller.

The other ad in the same vein was for the Renown double-decker, a considerably less successful model than the Reliance but one that is regarded by many as one of the best built in the 1960s. It was probably fated from the start, a front-engined model arriving too

London Transport have hit the bull's-eye with their Red Arrow service. The rapid transit, high density formula, which is used to move 5,000 commuters per vehicle per 5-day week, proves that AEC's rear engined bus design is right on target. More than 30 undertakings in the U.K. agree!

Swift: AH505 or AH691 underfloor diesel, 4 speed semi-automatic or fully automatic transmission. Wheelbases 16 ft. 6 in. and 18 ft. 6 in.

Commuta Mova!

AEC LTD · SOUTHALL · MIDDLESEX
Telephone: 01-574 2424

AEC

Above:

AEC was always proud of its London orders, and featured the Strachans-bodied AEC Swift in this 1968 advert.

late into a world that was moving toward rear engines. And while most Renown advertising was direct and effective the next example can't have helped its chances, even if hard-pressed transport managers had actually managed to plough through the copy.

It is another story-line. This time people waiting at a bus stop (in a 'lively provincial town with its bustling Saturday street-market crowds and queues of coast-bound cars') complain about the bus service. Or is it the traffic? 'Could we really blame the bus company for failing to put on more of its big, comfortable AEC double-deckers when none of the vehicles already in service could manage more than 10mph across town anyway?', the writer asks, and continues: 'The bus driver glanced across at us despairingly. His 75-seat bus looked half-empty — a big new AEC Renown with its handsome bodywork

designed to let it slide under country bridges that would stop any normal-height double-decker.' Fairly forcibly perhaps.

The story ends happily, of course, in a cloud of purple prose. 'Just then a murmur went up in the queue. A Renown was sweeping towards the kerb, its powerful 140bhp direct-injection diesel engine beating a welcome tattoo. A hiss as its power-operated doors slid open and we stepped aboard. The driver saw a gap in the traffic and we accelerated smartly away in air-suspended comfort. The Renown's efficient Monocontrol transmission took up smoothly but fast.'

Daimler on the other hand had a rather more straightforward approach to its advertising. It was one of the first manufacturers to list customers and orders, a throwback to the 1930s when this was a popular piece of one-upmanship. In fairness, Daimler had a good story to tell particularly when the Fleetline rear-engined double-decker came on stream in the early 1960s. By May 1962 it was able to announce orders from 10 municipalities and nine company fleets, and a year later those totals had grown to 16 and 14. In January 1963 it took a leaf out of Leyland's book, as we shall shortly see, and devoted a page to the news that '60% of all municipal bus tenders advertised during the last twelve months have resulted in orders for Daimler'.

But Daimler loses its way a bit with the Roadliner. Not just the chassis, the advertising. It starts with a two-page flourish in October 1964 ('only Daimler could make so outstanding a contribution to passenger transport') and with Daimler's solid reputation it seems that the Roadliner could well be a winner. Experience of course proved otherwise, and there is a sense of desperation in the frequency of Roadliner ads, mostly expensive double-page spreads, over the next

At times like these why pay more! MCW Metropolitan

All metal 45 seat luxury coach

£3,995

Inclusive of: Forced air ventilation. Ducted fresh air heating. Extra luggage locker. Chapman driver's seat. Windscreen washers. Mud flap.

Plus 2 years guarantee.

Try and beat that

mcw Metropolitan-Cammell-Weymann Limited, Elmdon Works, Marston Green, Birmingham

Above:
Prices were rarely mentioned in adverts and although MCW tried to change all that, it didn't do much for sales of the Metropolitan.

East Kent again buy Duple

One of a fleet of 49-passenger Express Coaches supplied to the East Kent Road Car Co. Ltd. by Duple.
Chassis: AEC Reliance

Duple Group Sales Ltd
The Hyde Hendon London NW9
01-205 6412
London Loughborough Blackpool

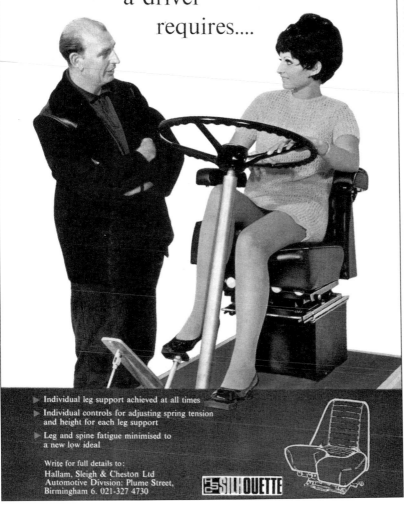

The seat with everything a driver requires....

▶ Individual leg support achieved at all times

▶ Individual controls for adjusting spring tension and height for each leg support

▶ Leg and spine fatigue minimised to a new low ideal

Write for full details to:
Hallam, Sleigh & Cheston Ltd
Automotive Division: Plume Street,
Birmingham 6. 021-327 4730

SILHOUETTE

Left:
East Kent orders were obviously prized, for manufacturers regularly featured East Kent buses, like this Duple-bodied AEC Reliance in 1968.

Above:
A touch of innuendo and an expanse of leg may have helped sell the Silhouette drivers' seat in 1968.

three years.

The confusion at Daimler is reflected in a curious series of Roadliner ads that actually started with No 2 ('Low-framed chassis allows step-free entrance and gangway'), and was followed by No 5 ('The ultra-compact power unit gives unrestricted layout') and No 6 ('Work-bench accessibility for easier maintenance'). Then the ads went back to No 2. We shall probably never ever find out what happened to ads 1, 3 and 4; maybe they covered reliability.

Daimler got back on the right track when it decided to go with the single-deck Fleetline rather than the Roadliner, and a series of ads pushed the benefits of standardisation where operators could have both double-deck and single-deck Fleetlines in service. The first 'Standardisation' ad used drawings, but later ads had photos of the real thing — single- and double-deck Fleetlines, side by side in the Halifax and Rochdale fleets.

The 1967 Transport Bill which led to the far-reaching 1968 Transport Act proposed a system of grants for new buses to specified layouts and Daimler was the only manufacturer to feature this in its advertising. Except of course when the odd desperate Roadliner ad was slipped in — Daimler was promoting the Roadliner right up to October 1969.

Leyland's approach was different again. Somebody in head office must have been a statistics freak, for record mileages, percentages and graphs litter the company's 1960s advertising. In between ads for the Atlantean, Leopard, Panther and Panther Cub, there are the statistical ads. 'More than 76% of all municipal operators now use Leylands', an ad announces in July 1964 and in case we don't believe it the ad goes on to tell us that 76.29% of municipal operators run Leylands, 40.5% of all municipally owned buses are Leylands, and 7,175 Leylands are in municipal service. The company changes tack in March 1965 ('3½ times more additional Leyland buses in municipal service than any other make') and again in May that year ('Leyland buses in municipal service now 41.83% — a post-war peak). Graphs are used to tell the same story in July 1965 comparing Leyland's 41.83% share of the municipal market with that of its nearest competitor at 23.95% and its second nearest competitor at 20.03%. A different statistic was used the following month ('Leyland municipal buses increased by 4.92%'), referring to the 1964 increase.

The strength of Leyland in municipal markets was undisputed, and it wisely chose not to highlight similar figures for the company fleets. By March 1966 the

Above:
Later Barton bodies were of a rather less striking appearance than the first rebuilds. This is a PS1 Tiger which was rebodied as shown here in 1955.

Below:
Attractive additions to the coach fleet in 1954 were five Alexander-bodied Leyland Tiger Cubs. Similarly-bodied AEC Reliances were also purchased. This style of body was rare outside Scotland.

Above:
In 1955 Barton made a bid for the business of Allen of Mountsorrel, following the death of its owner. In the event Midland Red took over the Allen business, but eight of the vehicles were purchased by Barton. These included two Willowbrook-bodied Daimler COG5/40s dating from 1939.

Below:
Some PS1s were rebodied as double-deckers. Nine had 61-seat Willowbrook bodies fitted in 1957. These were of conventional rear-entrance layout. New registrations disguised their origins.

Above:
As well as rebodying old single-deck chassis with new double-deck bodies, Barton did buy small numbers of new double-deckers. Two AEC Regent Vs with lowbridge Northern Counties bodies joined the fleet in 1957. One loads for Nottingham in Derby bus station in the spring of 1958.

Below:
Northern Counties was also chosen to rebody early postwar Leyland Tigers. In 1958/59 a total of 15 Tigers got new Northern Counties lowbridge bodies. Those delivered in 1959 were of full-front forward-entrance layout. As with earlier rebodies, these were re-registered, giving the impression of being brand-new buses rather than rebuilds.

Pig-snout and her younger sisters

Robert E. Jowitt with an occasional hesitation as to which designation fits which model, and some comparison with the career of Brigitte Bardot, traces the history of that popular postwar French bus, the Chausson.

'Ça n'aurait dû existé!' cried Monsieur Jean Robert. That should never have existed! These strong words of disapproval summed up the opinion of one of France's leading transport enthusiasts and a founder member of AMTUIR, the French public transport museum society, on the aesthetic qualities — or lack of them — of one of the most popular of French buses for two decades after World War 2 — the Chausson.

To say it was popular everywhere would not be true, but it was so widespread in both rural and urban operations that it left the contemporary Renaults and Berliets in the shade and the rest of the competition far behind. It was as Gallic as the 2CV Citroën, and indeed its bus equivalent by virtue of its cheap tin appearance and the love-hate feelings its inspired.

The firm of Chausson, based at Gennevilliers on a loop of the Seine northwest of Paris, was engaged in the manufacture of automobile radiators until 1939 it decided to branch out into integral-body coach construction. Not the best year to start such a venture, and if at this date any coaches were built it may be assumed they were soon crushed under the heel of the invader. The Chausson notion was probably sound enough, for French bus body design had been firmly

stuck in the 1920s until the mid-1930s when a few half-cabs and full-fronts began to oust the antique normal-control pattern. The war of course halted everything except trolleybus production, and this carried on the full-front theme. This concept was applied to all postwar buses, including the re-emerging Chausson.

Thus the first Chausson of 1946 had a front slightly 'V' in plan, leaning back at quite an angle, and fitted with a flush grille. It was equipped with a Hotchkiss petrol engine and designated 'AHE' meaning, we may hazard a guess, 'Autocar Hotchkiss Essence'. It was basically a country bus with a two-panel folding front door and, at the rear, a hinged emergency door which might be used unofficially at the terminus. The main attraction for operators, apart from the fairly novel idea of integral construction, was the cheap price allowed by the conception of mass production. Many examples went probably to rural operators, but a handful reached Le Havre for urban service, the authorities amidst the ruins of war obviously realising the truth of the adage 'Any port (or *Havre*) in a Storm'.

Above:
Original 1947-style *nez-de-cochon* Chausson with headlamps on brackets. This specimen seen in 1960 is working on the urban route from Clermont-Ferrand to Montferrand. ALL PHOTOGRAPHS BY THE AUTHOR

In 1947 the Hotchkiss petrol engine was superseded by a Panhard diesel, followed shortly afterwards by the alternative Somua diesel, and these versions were designated 'APH 47' and 'ASH 47'. Let us assume the 'H' indicated *huile* (diesel) and the '47' the year. To accommodate the larger engine, the

radiator now protruded from the flat front, giving rise to the nickname *nez-de-cochon* or pig-snout. French transport employees were ever ready with sobriquets for their charges; the Lyon double-deck trams were 'mothers-in-law', the Paris one-man Renaults of the 1930s were 'hen coops' and the bulbous-fronted 2D 2 electric loco-motives on the Paris-Orléans railway were 'pregnant women'. Paris, desperate for any vehicles with its fleet ravaged by Mars' depradations, took 18 pig-snouts, giving them

Top left:
Top left:
At the end of the 1940s the *nez-de-cochon* was modernised with flush headlights. Well over 20 years old in 1972, one of the last survivors speeds through Nantes on a gas and electric workers' service.

Middle left:
Autocars Granger of St Etienne was a great user of Chaussons on its interurban route 'CR' through a string of industrial villages to Rive de Gier. Here in the slums of St Etienne in 1960 are three generations of Chausson. On the left is the large-window model of the late 1950s, next to it the smaller-window earlier version and, flanked by two Isoblocs of other country operators, a *nez-de-cochon* with juke-box front bumpers c1950.

Bottom left:
The difference in the height of the windows — and the facial expression — between the APV, extreme left, and the APU type, all the rest, is plain to behold in this gathering of CNTC buses in Nantes in 1972. Note the destination board below the windscreen and the empty destination box.

fleet numbers 1-18, previously borne by the earliest 1916 Schneider 'H' models. If the Schneider had been so suitably Parisian that their style was maintained for two decades and their influence lasted another three-and-a-half, the Chaussons were as untypical as possible, lacking even the traditional route number box on the front roof.

This shortcoming was remedied on otherwise similar Nos 19-50 of 1948. Nos 51-54, 'APH 48' delivered in 1949, had a more dramatic improvement — this time in passenger flow — a two-panel folding door replacing the hinged rear door. In the same year Chausson improved the back of the bus by adding an extra window either side of the one small rear window of the early models, and the front by fitting the headlamps to the panel to replace the old-fashioned bracket-mounted type. These changes were marked by the designation 'APH 2.50' or 'ASH 2.50', even though they emerged in 1949. Paris, in 1950, took 18 such vehicles, which became Nos 55-72, and at the same time played about for several months with a version having a double-size four-panel rear entrance for city use with conductor enthroned over the rear axle; all previous buses having been one-man suburban vehicles. This specimen also

Right:
Saviem, after swallowing Chausson, kept on with the early design of 521 and 2.52, but with mesh grille and Saviem-style lettering, as shown on the bus on the right, replacing horizontal bars.

manifested some comfort for standing passengers, thanks to letter-box windows above the cant-rail affording some relief from an otherwise claustrophobically low ceiling. Despite, or because of, this essay Paris resolved for the moment to restrict the Chausson to the OMO suburbs.

Other cities had already proved perhaps less particular. For example, in 1947 Le Havre added the 'APH' to the 'AHE', in 1948 'APH' and 'ASH' began to replace the thoroughly dilapidated trams in Nancy, and the retreating streets of Metz or Clermont-Ferrand could be viewed through the single rear window. And if the original pig-snout was popular, the '2.50' became widespread in town use. Chausson offered doors and seating arrangements to suit the customer.

Such French transport history books as exist frequently contradict each other — and sometimes even themselves — so it is not wise to be too precise over designations, but we can safely say that pig-snouts flourished in Boulogne, Grenoble, Nantes, Nîmes and Nice, and be even more specific over Le Havre, Lyon, Marseille and Toulouse where they had three doors, with front and centre having two panels and rear having four, while Bordeaux was somewhat individual in having three doors all with two panels. Lyon's 15 specimens had standee windows like the Paris experiment and so did two of Marseille's 20. As for passengers, the range ran from 45 seated and 25 standing in Paris, to 16 seated and 74 standing in Le Havre.

Other towns beside those cited above undoubtedly ran pig-snouts too, and it might be almost impossible to count the country operators… Along the dykes in the morning mists in the flat landscape of the Nord and the Pas de Calais; in the grimy mining villages near the Belgian border where all the girls seemed to wear glasses; through the blooming orchards of Normandy where red-faced blue-eyed peasants tended panda-eyed cows; by the pine-edged creeks and rocky peninsulas where stocky fishermen spoke the Breton tongue, the pig-snout thrust its way. Over the wide cornfields of the Beauce; among the pleasant rolling

tiled villages of the lower Rhône and the endless vineyards of Languedoc where sturdy sun-tanned girls toiled, all this was Chausson country. More than in the streets and lanes of the cities amidst Second Empire boulevards and crumbling façades of antiquity, the Chausson was at home in the highways and hedges of rusticity. Hideously noisy and barbarically uncomfortable, a sweating driver with cigarette stuck in the corner of Gallic lips shaking hands with his passengers as he took their fares on frosty mornings or sunbaked hazy evenings, the *nez-de-cochon* was the essence of rural France.

Then came the new look.

It was about the same time, in 1952, that Brigitte Bardot first thrilled cinema audiences with a brief glimpse of nakedness in *Manina la fille sans voiles,* that the round-fronted Chausson thrilled transport operators. To say it was semi-circular in plan would

pastures of Touraine; by the winding sweet watered streams of Vienne and Charente; up into the barren heights and down into the rugged gorges of the Massif Central echoed the nez-de-cochon's lusty roar. Among the mysterious hills of the Vosges, through the pink-

be a gross exaggeration, but it almost gave that impression and it was certainly more curved than any contemporary bus. Even the windscreen looked curved though actually it was two large flat screens with two small flat corner screens. The rest of the body, except

Above:
A rural or suburban Chausson makes short work of overtaking a Lille tram amidst thoroughly northern French surroundings in 1961.

for the addition of a corrugated lower flank inspired perhaps by the 4CV van, was unchanged from the pig-snout, many examples until the end of production appearing without standee windows; but the front with an expressive countenance which could laugh or scowl was as up to date if never so attractive as Brigitte's pouts and smiles.

Paris started off evaluating half a dozen 521 'ASH' or 'AHH' (Somua or Hispano) and then took 60 'APH 2.52' (Panhard), a type which found favour from Lille to Biarritz via many places between, though Lyon and Marseille henceforth avoided the Chausson totally. Door arrangements varied from maximum three to the original one. However many you had, it was still basically a country bus.

This was remedied by the version known in Paris as the 'APU 53' (though in other places, confusingly, it seems to have been called the 'AHH'), in which the back was vertical with two large windows and two corner windows instead of the three across the earlier curving back. This allowed a large rear platform, which in the course of years started to sag. They were the only Chaussons to work on Paris city rather than suburban routes, and had a Wilson pre-selector gearbox. (Certain more cheeseparing operators stuck to the manual box.) Of 273 delivered to Paris, the later

ones had smooth flanks instead of corrugations. Among them fleet number 1111 was conspicuous, so too was Rouen's No 1.

At last, in 1956, as Bardot reached the height of fame in *Et Dieu Créa La Femme*, the decade-long problem of claustrophobia which — not withstanding standee windows — had bedevilled the Chausson was solved. The roof of what in Paris was known as the 'APVU' and elsewhere as 'APH 522' or 'ASH 522' was 17cm higher than that of the 'APU' The vehicles were recognisable by their higher and therefore more square windows and windscreens; the expressive face of the older generation was replaced by a bland smirk. The 'APVU' saw off the earlier Paris Chaussons but none managed to bag the magic fleet No 1 (which went to a new Berliet).

From 1956 to 1962 Paris acquired 756 'APVUs', variously OMO or conductored, generally for suburban use, in six series. The first readopted the corrugated bottom, thereafter abandoned. The third type had a far more drastic lapse from Paris fashion,

Isobloc and Floirat) so by 1962 later versions of the 'APVU' and '522' sported mesh grilles instead of bars; and the word Chausson in Saviem-style lettering ousted the old familiar winged device. The fusion resulted also in new designations, '522' becoming 'SC4', and it is pleasant to think that 'SC' stood for Saviem-Chausson; and worth noting that if the 'SC2' was basically a revamped Renault, it now displayed some Chausson touches. It can be argued that Chausson influence

forsaking the traditional route-number box. With the introduction of the round front, Chausson seemed to have forgotten the dimensions of an average destination blind, providing henceforth an enormous destination aperture frequently requiring a frame round the blind. In Nantes they used a tin board under the windscreen instead and left the destination box empty. Many rural operators did likewise. In Paris, however, they now discovered there was room to stuff number and destination blind side by side. This made the front more bland still; and worse was to follow.

It was a time of takeovers. The great General de Gaulle took over in France in 1958. A few years later the giant Saviem, formed in 1955 by uniting Renault, Somua and Latil, took over Chausson (as well as

survived far longer, for though the last 'SC4s' came off the production line incomplete in 1965, to be finished off by the ever-faithful Toulouse, the Standard 'SC10', which included Chausson-inspired integral construction, was to become the classic French urban bus for the next quarter century.

The Standard indeed successfully cleared the city streets of all Chaussons and by the end of the 1970s most country ones must have gone too. Some doubtless survived a while in non-psv use; the pig-snout had earlier been popular with showmen. If any exist now, however, it must surely be in scrapyards... except that Toulouse has preserved one, and even Jean Robert — who said they should never have existed, allowed a pig-snout from Bourges and the famous

Opposite top:
Beneath the walls of Rodez, Massif Central, in 1960, a Chausson of the firm of Bosquet, bound for Decazeville, 35 mountainous kilometres away. Alongside is a Panhard on a village service on to which that poor chap is definitely going to have to load all those tyres.

Opposite bottom:
This scene in Lille in 1961, apart from depicting remarkable consideration for the convenience of shoppers, displays an example of the widespread use of a basically rural bus on urban service. The mid-1950s Chausson on the sinister-sounding route X is noteworthy for its small-size Chausson device. This photo also emphasises how the windscreen of the rounded front was actually made up of flat glass.

Above:
Despite its popularity with urban as well as country users, the Chausson was never a true urban bus until the APU appeared in 1953. Here are some RATP Parisian examples at Gare de l'Est in 1969.

Left:
The city of Metz enjoyed many varieties of Chausson, from pig-snout through to the mesh-grille Saviem-badged versions of the SC4 seen here in 1969 by the 13th century cathedral of St. Etienne.

Paris No1111 to enter the sacred portals of the AMTUIR collection.

Well loved or vehemently hated, they were long a vital element of French transport and a typical slice of French life and landscape, and deserve a place in French social history equal to that which Brigitte acquired at the height of her popularity. If Bardot was the archetypal French girl, the *nez-de-cochon* and her younger sisters were the bus equivalent.

Left:
Rouen was ever faithful to Chausson, from pig-snout days to the end of production. Last in line in this 1974 view is a Saviem-Chausson SC4 type with Saviem-style grille over a latter-day version of the pig-snout on a rounded front to accommodate better front entrance facilities. Alongside is a Saviem Standard SC10, direct descendant of the Chausson by virtue of its integral construction, and the favourite French bus for the next quarter century. Behind is the church of St Ouen.

Right:
Just waiting in the rain in Le Havre in 1969, a *jeune fille* of almost Bardot grace watches a Chausson APV — only, lo and behold, it's a trolleybus! This 1960 motorbus look-alike was one of several in Le Havre with Vetra trolleybus equipment.

The disappearance of London Country

London Country Bus Services was one of the National Bus Company's biggest subsidiaries. It was split into four in the run-up to privatisation.
Kevin Lane illustrates some of what's happened since.

All change at London Country

London Country North West

January 1988	sold to its management
October 1990	acquired by Luton & District
February 1993	Slough depot and operations sold to Q Drive Buses
July 1994	Luton & District acquired by British Bus

London Country South West

February 1988	sold to Drawlane (now British Bus)
January 1993	renamed London & Country
January 1995	London operations reformed as Londonlinks

London Country South East

April 1987	renamed Kentish Bus & Coach Co
March 1988	sold to Proudmutual
July 1994	Proudmutual acquired by British Bus

London Country North East

April 1988	sold to AJS Group and Parkdale Holdings
January 1989	divided into two new companies, County Bus & Coach and Sovereign Bus & Coach
May 1990	Sovereign's Stevenage depot and operations sold to Luton & District
October 1990	control of County Bus & Coach passes to new Lynton Travel group
August 1991	Sovereign sold to Blazefield Holdings
October 1994	County Bus & Coach bought by West Midlands Travel

Left:
Kentish Bus expanded into London's red bus territory by winning London Transport contracts. New vehicles for these have in the main been Northern Counties-bodied Leyland Olympians, 56 of which were delivered in 1989/90.

Below:
London Country North East introduced a two-tone green livery as shown on a Metro-Cammell-bodied Atlantean in Enfield bus station in 1987.

Top:
LCNW added second-hand buses to its fleet including this one-time Selnec PTE Atlantean with Park Royal body. Note the addition of a North West logo to the standard NBC-style London Country fleetname.

Middle:
A new green and grey livery was developed for LCNW and continued after the takeover of the operation by Luton & District. A 1990 Carlyle-bodied Dennis Dart leaves Harrow for Watford Junction in 1991.

Bottom:
Among the older vehicles taken over by London Country South West was this ex-Barton Transport AEC Reliance, seen outside Addlestone garage in 1988. New in 1972, it had Plaxton bodywork.

Top:
Five Iveco minibuses with Robin Hood bodies joined the LCSW fleet in 1987. Two are seen in Horsham the following summer.

Bottom:
LCSW commissioned Ray Stenning's Best Impressions to develop a new look for the company. A distinctive two-tone green livery with a red stripe was the result, with the fleetname London & Country. A 1979 Roe-bodied Atlantean is followed by a B-series Leyland National in Surbiton in 1993.

Right:

Right:
All four London Country companies had an involvement in the Green Line coach operation. This anonymous LCNE Tiger heading through Kensington is on a Green Line service from London to Windsor.

Below:
Think half-cabs in relation to LCBS and you probably think Routemasters. But there were other types. Two Leyland Titan PD3As joined LCSW from Blackpool Transport for use as driver training buses. They were not operated as PSVs.

Thurgood of Ware

Geoff R. Mills traces the history of a small Hertfordshire coachbuilder.

The history of Thurgood coachworks, built in Ware, Hertfordshire, can be traced back to the years just after World War 1. It was in 1925 that the firm was founded by Walter L. Thurgood in premises formerly used as sawmills by the Phoenix Coach Works, where Mr Thurgood had been the foreman. One of his first contracts was jig and pattern work for his former employers before Phoenix went into voluntary liquidation.

The very first Thurgood-bodied bus was finished with plywood panelling on a 25cwt Morris chassis, produced as a fill-in job between other commitments. It found a buyer at Ketley Bank, near Warrington. A second project was a superior 14-seater built on a Chevrolet which was sold to a Northampton operator.

Encouraged by the success of the initial sales, work commenced on building a fleet of similar buses for the Peoples Motor Services which W. L. Thurgood started in 1927. The two-tone brown buses were busy throughout the Hertford district, serving Buntingford, Bishop's Stortford, Baldock, Epping, Hitchin, Royston

and Sawbridgeworth. The 21-vehicle fleet was garaged in premises alongside a new and much enlarged coachbuilding works in Park Road, Ware. The services together with the vehicles passed to the London Passenger Transport Board in December 1933, which enabled W. L. Thurgood to invest in yet another form of transport, while continuing to build bus bodies at the rate of two or three a month.

The new enterprise was Jersey Airways, operating a service from Portsmouth to St Aubin's Bay on Jersey with De Havilland Dragons built at Hatfield. A year

Above:
Thurgood's second bus body, built on a Chevrolet chassis. G. R. Mills collection

Top right:
One of the first postwar bodies was this 34-seater which was completed in February 1946 for Mulleys Motorways. The chassis was a prewar Gilford which had been new to Western SMT. It ran for Mulleys until 1959. The vertical cylinders below the headlamps are Gruss air springs. G. R. Mills

Right
Almost ready for delivery to Progressive Coaches of Cambridge in 1939, a former LPTB AEC Regal which had been rebodied by Thurgood. The nicely-proportioned body features a sliding sunroof. This is the Park Road works. G. R. Mills collection

later Guernsey Airways was registered, together with Channel Island Airways. A financial interest was retained until 1939 when a holding company gained control of the operations with the Great Western and Southern Railway companies securing 25% each.

Relieved of his airline interests, W. L. Thurgood was quick to see another area of business with development scope. He realised there was potential for the use of plastic laminated sheets beyond the coachbuilding trade and became a director of Warerite. This ingenious name for a product manufactured in Ware underlined that the new laminates would 'wear right' for the customer.

Orders within the transport world included lining the cocktail bar in the 'Coronation Scot' express carriages and the staterooms of Cunard's famed Queen Elizabeth liner. The business was sold to the giant American Bakelite group in 1940, with W.L.Thurgood

gaining shares in the controlling company.

Thurgood's coachbuilding operation gained momentum throughout the 1930s, with 1937 seeing the prewar peak when 43 chassis were bodied. Just under 400 bus bodies were built before the start of World War 2.

The war brought many problems, the worst blow happening in October 1940 when a high-explosive

bomb demolished the works. But after only five months the staff had rebuilt the main workshops and were actively engaged in the war effort, producing aircraft components such as jettison tanks for the De Havilland Mosquito. No new bus or coach bodies were built between March 1941 and late 1945.

Thurgood enjoyed a fair share of the postwar boom in coaching. Output more than doubled from 34 bodies in 1946 to 85 in 1947, and peaked at 90 in 1948 before falling back to 75 in 1949 and 40 in 1950.

In 1953 the company moved to new purpose-built premises at Widbury Hill, with considerably increased

facilities. Body production was now in single figures — except in 1955 when 10 were built — but the company was involved in repair work and was actively dealing in used psvs with a high concentration of customers in East Anglia and the West Country.

Low volume body production continued in the 1960s until in June 1967, after many months of

negotiation, the Thurgood coach business was sold to Plaxtons to form a southern area depot. Between 1946 and 1967 Thurgood had built a total of 439 bodies. Over the years it had bodied most makes of chassis including AEC, Albion, Austin, Bedford, Commer, Crossley, Daimler, Dennis, Dodge, Gilford, Guy, Leyland, Maudslay, TSM and Thornycroft.

The sale of the coach building and dealing businesses left W. L. Thurgood Ltd as a property holding company owning a BBC stores building and a petrol station on sites adjoining the coachworks.

Top left:
Thurgood built bodies on a small number of mid-engined chassis, as shown by this 1951 Leyland Royal Tiger in the Eastern National fleet. The coach was built for a rather smaller Chelmsford operator, Rose Bros which traded as Primrose. The use of a sliding door on a front-entrance coach was unusual. G. R. Mills

Bottom left:
The arrival of mid-engined chassis virtually killed off the old front-engined models overnight. However, as late as the summer of 1952 Cannon's of Puckeridge, Hertfordshire, took this 35-seat body on a Guy Arab III chassis — their second such coach. The full-width front added a touch of modernity to an obsolete concept. G. R. Mills

Above:
Tilling-Stevens chassis were on the way out when this lightweight L4MA8 was built in 1952 — which was in fact the last year of Tilling-Stevens production. Powered by a 98bhp four-cylinder Meadows engine, this 37-seater was another coach for Rose Bros of Chelmsford. It is seen in 1962 in the ownership of Sorrell of Hatfield Peverel. G. R. Mills

Below:
Not quite what they seem. Both bodies were built by Thurgood in 1960 (and represent 50% of that year's output) — but while the coach furthest from the camera is a brand new Bedford SB1, that nearest the camera is in fact a Dennis Lancet which had just been rebodied. The operators were respectively Lees Luxury of Barnet and Modern Super of Enfield, both part of the Horseshoe Coaches group of Tottenham, North London. G. R. Mills

Above:
Latterly production concentrated on smaller coaches. This 28-seat bus with a body style which was known as the Forerunner was one of six bodies of this design built in 1963 which represented the year's entire output. The others had coach seats. New to Bream of Hemel Hempstead, it was built on a Ford 530E chassis, an unusual choice for a bus of this size. G. R. Mills

Below:
Thurgood's last body was this 29-seat Successor, supplied to Elms Coaches of Kenton in July 1967. It is seen prior to delivery, ready to enter service with its F-registration on 1 August — 1967 was the first year when the registration suffix changed on 1 August instead of 1 January. The chassis was a Bedford VAS5. G. R. Mills

SOUTH WALES SAFARI

In the 1950s and 1960s South Wales offered an amazing variety of buses and operators. **Alistair Douglas** looks back.

Below:
It's 1953 and an elegant AEC Regal of Cardiff Corporation awaits its tour of duty. New in 1937, it had a Northern Counties body. It was withdrawn in 1956. The 1937 Regals were Cardiff's last half-cab single-deckers. ALL PHOTOGRAPHS BY THE AUTHOR

Below: In 1959 there was still plenty to see in Barry Island coach park. In this superb line-up the three Red & White coaches nearest the camera are all AEC Regal IIIs new to Ralphs of Abertillery. One, dating from 1948, has Duple coachwork while the other two have Barnard bodies and were new in 1950. All are smartly turned out, despite their age.

Left:
Elsewhere in the Barry Island coach park was this unusual Leyland Tiger operated by Jones of Aberbeeg. It had been new in 1949 to Silcox of Pembroke Dock, who built the body themselves.

Below left:
Red & White and United Welsh operated large numbers of Albions. A 1948 CX13 with Lydney body stands in Chepstow in 1959. Within a few years the type would have disappeared.

Top right:
Cardiff's trolleybuses were still alive and well in 1962 and the fleet included a few single-deckers. This three-axle BUT has East Lancs bodywork. It was one of five delivered in 1949. Cardiff's last trolleybus ran in January 1970.

Middle:
Newport frequently bought buses unlike those elsewhere in the country. One such oddity was this Dennis Falcon with bodywork by Davies. It was new in 1954 and was the only Falcon — of this generation — to be operated by a British municipality.

Bottom right:
Merthyr Tydfil bought several batches of Bristols until nationalisation of the chassis maker forced the operator to source its new vehicles elsewhere. This is a K6A of 1945 with a much-rebuilt Park Royal body. It survived until 1964.

Left:
Pontypridd was another Bristol user. This, too, is a 1945 Park Royal-bodied K6A which was set to have a particularly long life, running until 1967.

Below left:
Gelligaer Urban District Council had a distinctive livery of green, red and grey and its fleet consisted mainly of single-deckers. This AEC Regent III, one of a pair purchased in 1949, had a Bruce lowbridge body and was photographed in Hengoed in 1962. At that time there were just five double-deckers in the 28-strong fleet.

Top right:
By 1962 the Bedford OWB was almost extinct as a psv, although many survived as mobile shops. This one was still active with Brewer of Caerau.

Right:
Bebb of Llantwit Fardre was one of three independents operating local services around Pontypridd as Amalgamated Bus Services. A Burlingham-bodied Crossley coach was running on one of those services in 1962.

Top left:
Llynfi of Maesteg was, and still is, a well-known independent. Here a 1947 Leyland Tiger PS1 with a 1957 Neath body hurries homeward through Bryn, followed by a Massey-bodied Daimler.

Bottom left:
The associated companies Kenfig Motors and Porthcawl Omnibus Co ran a number of local services. A former Sunderland District Roe-bodied Leyland PD1 is seen in Porthcawl.

Above:
South Wales Transport ran a predominantly AEC fleet. A 1953 Regent III/Weymann is followed by a 1961 Bridgemaster in this 1962 view.

If this is Thursday...

Round the World in 80 days? **Stewart J. Brown** beats that by a handsome margin.

preferred Father Christmas job, but it looked a lot more attractive than working six days a week and having Sunday off.

But, no, that wasn't to be either. Editing *Buses Yearbook* looked like an attractive alternative. Work one month a year and have the other 11 off. Until you discover that to keep body and soul together the other 11 have to be worked too.

Freelance writing beckoned, and thus it came to pass that by 1994 my multifarious activities included writing not just about buses but — shock, horror — about trucks, too. They've got a fair amount in common with buses, such as engines and, in some cases, axles and gearboxes. However, fear not, I'm not about to explain the mysteries of such delights as Scania R113s or Volvo FL6s — I realise N113s and B6s have much more appeal in these pages.

Now, the reason for explaining all this — and there is a reason, as you will shortly find — is that in 1994 alongside my bus writing I was editing a magazine about trucks called *Trucking International*. So what, you ask? Well,

L aziness is not some form of original sin. In fact, worked up to an art form it can have quite a lot going for it. Not that I'm lazy, of course — just economical of effort.

When I was a child I fancied Santa Claus's job. One day's work. 364 days' holiday. Not a bad deal. Gradually, I realised that this wasn't an attainable goal. My thoughts turned to the church. Why not become a man of the cloth? Work every Sunday; have six days off. It clearly required 52 times more effort than my

being a magazine editor opens all sort of doors, including on occasion those into airport departure lounges. This in turn can lead to flights to far-flung places.

Which is where this story really takes off, if you'll pardon the pun.

Scania, while it may not be big in buses in Britain, is a worldwide operation selling trucks and buses in all

Top left:
Surprise find: trolleybuses in São Paulo.
ALL PHOTOGRAPHS BY THE AUTHOR

Left:
Biggest fleet: Cometa run 1,000 near-identical Scania coaches.

Above:
Mighty Merc: small buses like this provide the bulk of Buenos Aires' bus services.

sorts of far-off lands. And it decided that one way to get this message home to a select few editors who might not be fully aware of this was to take them to some.

The trip which beckoned was the one which took Phileas Fogg 80 days: around the world.

Day 1: After abandoning my car at London's Heathrow Airport, the journey starts, appropriately enough, on a Scania — an N113 with Van Hool body on the car-park shuttle service. Its next stop is Terminal 4. Mine is São Paulo.

Day 2: It's an overnight flight — set off at 22.15, arrive in Brazil many hours later at 05.45 local time.

For the Brazilians meeting us it is the crack of dawn, for the small group of exhausted editors and their hosts from Scania it's mid-afternoon. And just

Above: **World's end: Patagonian Mercedes at Rio Gallenos.**

Below: **It's a gas: one of Sydney's gas-powered Scanias.**

the first of many challenges coming to our biological clocks and dual-time watches.

A suicidal Brazilian minibus driver gets us to the centre of one of the world's biggest cities without hitting anything — but only just. Brazilian drivers are all would-be racing-car champions.

Sâo Paulo's first surprise is the existence of trolleybuses, conveniently running on a route past our hotel's front door. Like most trolleybuses they were soulless and anonymous, but it is a long time since I have seen a trolley, so they get a second glance. Motorbuses are mainly locally-built dual-door Mercedes, with a number of full-size Volkswagen buses, also of local manufacture. You didn't know that VW made full-size buses? That makes two of us.

One of the reasons for visiting Brazil is that it houses a Scania truck and bus plant and is one of the company's biggest markets. It is also home to the world's biggest Scania operator, a coach company called Cometa which runs almost 1,000 K112s and K113s on

Above:
Old and new: Ventura Reo alongside K93.

Left:
Aussie Atlantean: smart ex-Sydney PDR1 with Kingsgrove Bus & Coach.

115

Scania and a US-built GMC but, sadly, none of an even earlier generation still which included AECs, or ACLOs as they were known here. Spot a mysterious red left-hand drive double-decker in a scrapyard, but no time to stop. This is work, remember.

There's a Metro in the city too. Now, I'm not a timid traveller, but when the hotel receptionist advises removing my rings and watch before descending below ground I think better of it. Anyway, the whole trip is being run on a tight schedule and it means more time for bus photography.

express services radiating from São Paulo. Cometa not only runs the services, but it builds its own bodies, which are modelled loosely on a mid-1950s North American design. All 1,000 of its coaches are virtually identical, with only detail design improvements to distinguish the newest from the oldest. And all are immaculate.

Which is more than can be said for their home city which, in places, is a shade run-down. Cometa has a fine sense of its history and has kept a couple of earlier-generation coaches including a front-engined

Top:
Murrays midi: Mitsubishi Rainbow carries luggage in a trailer.

Above:
National Bus: New owner's name above driver's side window on Melbourne Volvo.

Above: **Super tram: classic Melbourne transport.**

Below: **Rare Dennis: one of KMB's 300-plus Jubilants.**

Day 3: Fly to Manaus in the Amazonian rain forest. Observe there's a lot of rain forest about, after flying over it for three solid hours. Buses in Manaus are mainly locally-built Marcopolos, but with no clue as to what lies underneath the body. Suspect a front-engined Mercedes chassis.

Day 4: No buses, no flying. River trip on the Amazon in a double-deck wooden boat. Note that it is Scania-powered.

Day 5: No buses, more flying — back for a night in São Paulo.

Day 6: No buses, lots of flying, firstly to remote parts of Brazil where soya beans are harvested. Oh yes, and transported. In Scanias, amongst other types of truck.

Back to São Paulo and then immediately on to another plane — bound for Buenos Aires. Start to get withdrawal symptoms. Haven't photographed a bus since Day 2. Which might seem a bit odd in the country which is the world's largest bus market and buys more Scanias than anywhere else in the world — sales of Scanias in Brazil averaged over 1,000 a year in 1992 and 1993.

Day 7: Arrive in the Argentinian capital at 01.50. Not sure if we're in a different time zone or not. Some airport clocks give different times from others. It's all very confusing.

Collapse in a hotel at some ungodly hour, but sleep

doesn't come easy. Buenos Aires has always been high on my list of places to visit and there's a real sense of excitement. I'm here! Pinch myself to make sure.

Up at dawn (well, dawn-ish) and out to see Buenos Aires' buses. We're only here for a little over 24 hours, so I've got to make the most of it.

The city is served in the main by bonneted Mercedes, built on what are essentially truck chassis. They're colourful. They're busy. And they're everywhere. They're also of indeterminate age but, I suspect, not as old as they look. A bit like me, really. Find one of the city's main railway stations, a grand Victorian edifice which wouldn't look out of place in any European city. But the station is more interesting than the trains, which prove to be modern and not too exciting.

Photograph a dmu while wondering if Argentina is one of those places where officials get a bit twitchy if you photograph trains. Slink out of the station without being arrested, so obviously it's not.

Day 8: An early start to see some Scania truck operators. Early starts characterise the timetable wherever we are. Then at midday onto the longest flight yet. It heads south to the tip of South America,

Below:
Alexander export: air-conditioned R-type on tri-axle Olympian.

Right:
Oriental Ikarus: rush-hour traffic in downtown Taipei.

118

landing in a God-forsaken airport in the middle of a lunar landscape. If anyone ever offers you a free weekend in Rio Gallenos, my advice is to politely decline.

Our stop is only a couple of hours while the 747 is refuelled, but it's quite adequate to take in the atmosphere — and Rio Gallenos airport boasts three buses. Two are the Patagonian Bus Co's bonneted Mercedes standing outside what passes for the international terminal, the third is an altogether more luxurious Scania K93 coach which just happens to be waiting for its passengers. Armed police blow whistles at transit passengers with cameras who stray too far from the terminal.

Late afternoon we take off and head into the setting sun. Our next stop is Sydney — with a change at Auckland on the way.

Day 9: No buses, and lots and lots of flying. In fact, Day 9 disappears. We left Argentina at 17.00 on Day 8. Somewhere on the trip we crossed the international dateline, losing a day of our lives, and many hours and a change of plane later, we reach Sydney at midnight, which is the start of Day 10. Bus withdrawal symptoms threaten again.

Day 10: A midnight finish after a flight half-way round the southern hemisphere doesn't daunt Scania. We're on the road at 08.00. (No, it's OK, I'll skip breakfast.) But here are real buses. Spot an ex-Sydney Atlantean in the ownership of Kingsgrove, a private operator. Snatch a photograph by hanging out of the car. My fellow travellers suspect that travel exhaustion must be getting to me. Why else would anyone photograph a double-deck bus from a moving car when there are thousands of the things back home?

Visit the State Transit Authority which has a big gas bus programme, using — surprise, surprise — Scania L113s with smart looking 49-seat bodywork by Ansair.

The gas-powered engine offers performance which is broadly comparable with a diesel, but noticeably quieter. The exhaust emissions are cleaner too, which is the whole point of the exercise. The only operational minus point is the weight penalty — around one tonne — incurred in fitting gas cylinders in place of a diesel tank.

This concern about clean efficient public transport seems a long way removed from deregulated Britain — what am I saying? It *is* a long way removed from deregulated Britain.

Then on to Murrays Coaches, a high-class operation which runs Mitsubishi Rainbow midis and full-sized Scanias with air-conditioned PMC bodies. Owner Ron Murray has a computerised booking and control system which is second to none. And the coaches are pretty damned impressive too. Coach operations as professional as this are a joy to behold.

After dark, think I'm hallucinating when I see a Sydney PD2 Titan in the street. Rub my eyes in disbelief, then discover it's on some sort of nostalgia run. Have no camera but after 10 days of non-stop travel am getting my first and only attack of fatigue and decide that when you've seen one Sydney PD2

you've seen them all. Which may, of course, be true. For half-an-hour in the evening feel that death would be a welcome release. But soon recover.

Decide Sydney is a wonderful city. Magnificent new buildings. Wonderful old buildings. Manchester meets Manhattan. It's even better than Buenos Aires. And there's no need to avoid arguments about the ownership of Las Malvinas.

Day 11: More flying, no buses — well not unless you count the Murrays Mitsubishi Rainbow which whisks us to the airport at 07.00. Two flights and four hours later touch down in Port Augusta on the edge of the outback. Still no buses, but the trucks — twin-trailer roadtrains — are mighty impressive. One more

flight and we're back in Adelaide — but it's 19.00 and it's dark. Imagine getting to a city on the other side of the world and not being able to photograph a single bus. It's frustrating, but that's my experience of Adelaide. Don't ask me what colour Adelaide's buses are. I didn't actually see any in daylight.

Day 12: It's 06.00 and it's still dark and we're off to catch a flight to Melbourne. Wonder if it's always dark in Adelaide. At 09.00 we're touring Scania Australia's Melbourne assembly plant which, among

Below:
Neoplan look-alike: Taiwanese-built body for Scania coach.

other things, puts together Dennis Dart chassis for the Australian market.

Then off to Ventura, a loyal Leyland operator whose fleet includes Leopards and modern Tigers. Following Leyland's demise, Ventura switched to Scania's K93 and these, with 39-seat dual-door Volgren bodywork, now form the front-line fleet. The company has a sense of heritage and instead of going out for a spin in a sparkling new K93, an immaculately-restored 1928 Reo is coaxed into life and taken out for a head-turning run.

Ventura brings back memories of all that was best in independent bus operators in Britain 30 years ago. A smart fleet. Nice premises. Everything clean and tidy. A bit like McGill's of Barrhead. Or perhaps Fishwick's of Leyland.

Back into central Melbourne, and a couple of hours to look round. Melbourne's older buses have distinctive bodywork with flat glass screens. Most seem to be Volvos, while newer vehicles are MANs. A change of ownership is taking place and some vehicles carry National Bus Company fleetnames on Melbourne's green and yellow livery. No time to ride on a bus but I hop on a tram just for the hell of it.

Day 13: Decide Australia isn't a bad place. In fact it's pretty good — pity it's so far away. But Day 13 is set to be another of those lost days. No buses. More flying. We're on the road at 08.00 and in the air at 11.00. Our destination? Hong Kong.

It's late evening when the Cathay Pacific Jumbo Jet touches down, with its wing tips passing so close to the flats which crowd round the airport that you can actually look in. It's quite uncanny. The minute the cabin doors open the heat and a pungent smell waft in. Welcome to Hong Kong.

Day 14: Hong Kong has long been a Mecca for British bus enthusiasts with its history of double-deck operation. But our stay here is brief — less than 24 hours. So, as in Buenos Aires I'm up at the crack of dawn. The day has another early start and I forgo breakfast (which has now become a habit to this confirmed late riser) to snatch a few pictures of KMB buses outside the hotel, which is conveniently near a bus station. See Guy Victorys, a few of the 40-odd surviving Daimler Fleetlines, Dennis Dragons and Darts, MCW Metrobuses, some air-conditioned Leyland Olympians. It's exciting. But even at 07.30 with the sun not long up it's hot. Find that some of what appear to be Dennis Darts are in fact Mitsubishis.

We're in Kowloon, which means no chance to see Hong Kong's trams or CMB's buses. Can you believe it? In Hong Kong and not a single CMB picture to show for it.

Between truck operators we squeeze in a short visit to the headquarters of KMB, adjacent to the company's unique multi-storey bus garage. KMB runs 3,200 buses — and two of them are tri-axle N113s.

Hong Kong isn't good Scania bus territory. Dennis and Volvo (with Olympians) rule the roost.

Everything about KMB is big — it runs 300 routes, has 6,000 drivers (or bus captains) and carries 19 million passengers a week.

But by mid-afternoon it's back to the airport. The if-this-is-Hong-Kong-it-must-be-Thursday feeling is really taking over. All airports are beginning to look the same. Hong Kong's just has longer queues.

It's late when we touch down in Taipei.

Day 15: It would be wrong to judge Taiwan by impressions of Taipei. But it has to be said that Taipei has little to commend it. It's noisy, dirty, crowded, hot. There's a madding crowd, but you can't get far from it. Suddenly the austere charm of Rio Gallenos seems quite appealing.

Taiwan's urban buses are an odd mixture of Japanese Hinos and Hungarian Ikaruses. There are plenty of them, but the sheer volume of traffic makes photography difficult. The city's buses jostle for space with taxis and scooters. It's pandemonium. There's a Metro in build (Rail, not Rover). From my hotel balcony I take a quick picture of a train on test on an overhead section of track.

Inter-city coaches are Scanias with locally built bodywork which is a fair copy of Neoplan's Jetliner. Come the afternoon it's a relief to step on a plane back to Hong Kong, the first leg of the long flight home. Day 15 ends with lift off from Hong Kong in a westward-bound Jumbo.

Day 16: It's a few minutes before 06.00. We're back. We've made 19 flights. Been to five countries in three continents. Spent 72 hours in the air — that's three days of our lives in flight. We're exhausted — and exhilarated too.

With a fitting symmetry the journey ends as it began, on another Scania on the airport car-park service. I then go to my office to clear up two week's mail — before going home and indulging in one of my favourite pastimes: sleep. It takes up some 30 hours out of the next 48. And it's sound.

I hate the phrase 'once in a lifetime' to describe a trip, but can think of no other. I've been to many far-flung places, but always on an out-and-back trip. It was my first visit to each of the countries involved, and my first complete circumnavigation of the globe.

And, yes, it was a once in a lifetime experience. I doubt very much if I'll fly round the world again — although I'm always open to offers. But no early starts please. I'm an owl, not a lark.

United we stand

Lancashire United Transport built up a reasonably big coach fleet from the 1950s, but often with an idiosyncratic choice of vehicles.
Reg Wilson illustrates a selection.

LUT's postwar coaches

1951	10 Guy Arab III/Roe
1952	7 Guy Arab UF/Roe
1953	6 Leyland Tiger TS8/Plaxton rebody
1957	5 Leyland Tiger Cub/Duple (Midland)
1958	5 Leyland Tiger Cub/Duple (Midland)
1959	5 AEC Reliance/Burlingham
1960	8 Leyland Tiger Cub/Northern Counties
1961	8 AEC Reliance/Plaxton
1962	8 AEC Reliance/Plaxton
1963	6 AEC Reliance/Plaxton
1964	8 Leyland Leopard/Plaxton
1965	8 Leyland Leopard/Plaxton
1966	4 Leyland Leopard/Plaxton
1969	4 Leyland Leopard/Plaxton
1974	5 Leyland Leopard/Plaxton
1977	5 Leyland Leopard/Plaxton
1978	5 Leyland Leopard/Plaxton
1979	4 Leyland Leopard/Plaxton
1980	3 Volvo B58/Plaxton

Above:
LUT's first true coaches were 10 Guy Arab IIIs, bought in 1951 at a time when most operators had switched to underfloor-engined chassis. They had 35-seat Roe bodies and wore the company's red livery but with black relief for the wings and roof. They were LUT's last half-cab single-deckers and survived until the mid-1960s. This one is seen in Liverpool in 1956 on a football hire.
REG WILSON

Above and Below;
The Arab IIIs were followed in 1952 by the company's first underfloor-engined vehicles, which included seven relatively uncommon Arab UFs, again bodied by Roe. The stepped waistline helped give these centre-entrance 39-seat coaches a distinctive appearance. When new, they carried the same red and black livery as the Arab IIIs, but they were later repainted in a brighter red and cream style.
REG WILSON

Top left:
The coach fleet, now numbering 17, was further expanded in 1953. But instead of buying new vehicles, LUT had half-a-dozen prewar Leyland Tiger TS8s fitted with new full-front coach bodies by Plaxton. They looked like new vehicles, and for those in the know only the 1939 Lancashire registration gave the game away. They were withdrawn in 1960.

Left:
A four-year gap followed the TS8s, before the arrival in 1957/58 of 10 Leyland Tiger Cubs with Duple Donnington bodies. These all-metal bodies were produced in Loughborough by Duple (Midland) and were of a rather more austere appearance than Duple's Hendon-built coaches. They were to be LUT's only Duple-bodied coaches.
REG WILSON

Above:

In 1961 LUT switched to new Plaxton-bodied coaches for the first time — and stayed loyal to the Scarborough company from then on. However, instead of specifying the trendsetting Panorama, the model chosen was the dual-purpose Highway. LUT took 16 coaches of this type in 1961-62, all on AEC Reliance chassis. REG WILSON

Below:

The coaches delivered in 1963/64 were all of the new 11m maximum length, with a comfortable 45 seats (the norm was 49) instead of the 41 of earlier 30ft-long vehicles. The 1963 coaches were AECs (the fleet's last Reliances); the 1964 vehicles, as seen here in Manchester, were LUT's first Leyland Leopards. The 11m Highway body had no fewer than eight side windows while the contemporary Panorama had but four. Note the route number blind, for use on express services. REG WILSON

Above:
Real coaches at last! In 1965 eight short L2 Leopards were delivered with the latest style of Plaxton's popular Panorama body. These introduced a smart new grey and red livery to the company's coach fleet.
REG WILSON

Right:
The Leopard/Plaxton combination became LUT's standard for the remainder of the 1960s and the 1970s. In 1969 four PSU4s were added to the coach fleet. These had the new Panorama Elite body, with slight curvature in the side windows.
REG WILSON

Below:
LUT was taken over by Greater Manchester Transport in 1976 and new coaches in 1977 wore a version of GMT's standard coach livery with its upswept stripes. The base colour was white and, for LUT, the stripes were red and yellow. Note that the waist moulding on this Plaxton-bodied PSU3 has been broken to accommodate the upsweep of the stripes above the rear wheels.
REG WILSON

Bottom:
LUT's last coaches broke with tradition. After evaluating the latest Leopard model alongside Volvo's B58, the Swedish-built chassis won, and three joined LUT in 1980. The last time a foreign-built chassis had been bought by LUT was in 1923. The last of the Volvos, No 616, brought to an end the new fleet number series started by a Burlingham-bodied Reliance 21 years earlier. In 1981 LUT was absorbed into the main GMT fleet. REG WILSON